THE TRUE STORY OF NOTORIOUS ARIZONA OUTLAW AUGUSTINE CHACÓN

THE TRUE STORY OF NOTORIOUS ARIZONA OUTLAW AUGUSTINE CHACÓN

DAVID GRASSÉ

FOREWORD BY MARK BOARDMAN,
EDITOR OF *THE TOMBSTONE EPITAPH*

THE History PRESS

Published by The History Press
Charleston, SC
www.historypress.com

Cover image: Augustine Chacón. *Arizona Historical Society, PC 1000, Main Photo Collection, Portraits—Chacón, Augustine, #29909.*

First published 2021

Manufactured in the United States

ISBN 9781467147965

Library of Congress Control Number: 2021938513

Notice: The information in this book is true and complete to the best of our knowledge. It is offered without guarantee on the part of the author or The History Press. The author and The History Press disclaim all liability in connection with the use of this book.

For all those who are unjustly maligned.

CONTENTS

FOREWORD

"When the legend becomes fact, print the legend."

That line from *The Man Who Shot Liberty Valance* has become almost cliché over the years. It could apply to almost every notable character of the Old West. Often, the legends started while the principal was still alive, the creation of liberty-taking journalists who were more interested in good storytelling than in the truth.

And then, over time, others just repeated the tales, not bothering to check out what really did (or did not) happen. Very flesh-and-blood people like Wyatt Earp, Jesse James and Billy the Kid were magically transformed into larger-than-life figures, men whose exploits were greater than those of most normal humans—faster on the gun, nervier in the toughest situations, cannier at the gambling tables, more successful with the ladies and so on.

Mexican bandit Augustine Chacón got that treatment over the decades. Reputedly, he was a brutal and deadly force on both sides of the United States–Mexico border in the years surrounding 1900. He and his gang supposedly ran rampant over southeast Arizona. Some chroniclers claim that Chacón was involved in up to forty-two killings, a remarkable number for anybody in any era. In a nearly Christ-like episode, he was betrayed by a friend and sent to the gallows. There, the outlaw exhibited incredible courage and calm in the face of death.

It's a great story. Just one problem: most of it is pure fantasy. And that's where David Grassé comes in. Over the past fifty years, more and more historians have examined the Old West legends and found them wanting. The truth is simpler and, in some ways, less exciting than the legends. The Wyatt Earps and Billy the Kids were real people, who did good and bad and a lot of everyday things that make no difference and deserve little or no notice. Augustine Chacón fits that category as well, as Grassé shows in this examination of the bandit.

I won't spoil things before we get to the heart of the matter. But let's just say that Augustine Chacón was the victim of a white newspaper and legal establishment that turned a minor bad man into the embodiment of evil. And then succeeding generations of quasi-historians and storytellers just regurgitated those tales, without checking to see if they were true or not. Not so David Grassé. He has taken the time and effort, observing information with a critical eye, to get at the facts. Augustine Chacón was a minor character in turn-of-the-century Arizona Territory. And in presenting the facts, Grassé has done everyone a favor. Now we have the history at hand.

Will this book erase all the lies told about Chacón over the past 130 years? No way. But now we can compare them to the facts. Yes, when the legend becomes fact, print the legend. That's just the way of things. But for those who want a bit more than myth and legend, the truth is out there, discovered and told by real historians like David Grassé. This is the true story of Augustine Chacón. No legend, just fact.

MARK BOARDMAN
Senior Editor,
The Tombstone Epitaph

ACKNOWLEDGEMENTS

I would like to take a moment to extend my thanks to the many people who made it possible for me to do the work I do:

Laurie Krill, Ryan Finn, Crystal Murray and the folks at The History Press.

Mark Boardman, senior editor of *The Tombstone Epitaph*.

Wendy Trakes, Sara Guzman, Laura Blandford and the entire crew of archivists and research librarians at the Arizona State Library and Archives in Phoenix.

Ms. Rachel Black and the staff at the Arizona Historical Society.

Nancy Liliana Godoy, associate archivist of Chicanx Research Collection, Arizona State University Library, Distinctive Collections.

Matt Messbarger, archivist, Arizona State University Library, Distinctive Collections.

Edres Bryant Barney, curator and manager at the Eastern Arizona Museum & Historical Society in Pima, Arizona.

Barb Keely at the Pinal County Historical Society.

Sean Harrington, reference/electronic resources librarian, Ross-Blakley Law Library, Arizona State University.

Ms. Valerie Kittle at the Postal History Foundation, Tucson.

Ms. Kathy Klump at the Sulphur Springs Valley Historical Society.

All those persons who have purchased and read my earlier books, which has had the effect of encouraging me to continue writing these histories of the Arizona Territory and the inhabitants thereof.

And, of course, my sister, Erin, and my mother, Geraldine, who have never wavered in their support of my creative endeavors.

My apologies, as I am certain I forgot someone.

A thing is not necessarily true because a man dies for it.

—Oscar Wilde

CHAPTER 1

A DUBIOUS BEGINNING

The Mexican outlaw Augustine Chacón has become something of legend—*un hombre muy malo*—with a veritable litany of crimes and depredations attributed to him, most of which are complete fictions. These fictions, which began to envelop Chacón during his lifetime, have continued to be reiterated, as though they were factual, well into the modern era. Like the legend that surrounds the mythic Californio social bandit Joaquin Murrieta that originated with the 1854 novel by John Rollins Ridge, the legend of Augustine Chacón is almost exclusively the invention of contemporary, Anglo-American newspaper editors. The various stories of murder, rape, robbery and other atrocities allegedly committed by Chacón served to elevate him from a common criminal to an outlaw of renown—a veritable legend in his own time. Of course, it became necessary, once Chacón had been raised to the status of a near-mythic figure, to make an example of him.

These period tales reflect the underlying xenophobia and racist mindset of the majority of the Anglo-American population in the southwestern territories who believed, steadfastly, in their own moral and cultural superiority. The crimes of Augustine Chacón, though blatant fabrications, served to reinforce the prevailing and pervasive racialist/racist ideas concerning the innate degeneracy of persons of other ethnicities, especially those of Hispanic and indigenous ancestry. The Anglo newspapermen turned Chacón into a villainous archetype, embodying all their racist beliefs about the dissoluteness and depravity of the Hispanic peoples.

The town of Morenci, Arizona Territory, circa 1883. *Phelps Dodge pictures, courtesy of the Greenlee County Historical Society.*

The elevation of Chacón by the territorial press—and, in turn, by the national press—to the status of a celebrity criminal, his trial and his subsequent execution by the Anglo-American judicial establishment were meant to be understood as a cautionary tale to all persons of Hispanic heritage living within the territory. The hanging of Augustine Chacón was, for all intents and purposes, a legal lynching, serving to remind the Hispanic population of their permanently inferior status within the Anglo-American sociopolitical construct and guaranteeing their continuing acquiescence. Those persons who were not accepting of this paradigm, and those who challenged or defied it, would be dealt with in the harshest manner, just as Chacón was.

In point of fact, Augustine Chacón did not even rate a mention in the territorial press until December 1895. On the seventeenth of said month, at about 12:30 a.m., it was reported that two "Mexican" men had broken into Mrs. McCormick's mercantile in the town of Morenci by crawling through a window in the rear of the store. The German-born clerk, Paul Becker, had gone to dinner about a half an hour earlier, locking up the store behind him. When he returned, he was surprised by "two masked men," one armed with a revolver and the other armed with a knife. Becker attempted to resist his assailants and was clubbed in the forehead by the man with the pistol. The robbers then restrained him physically and went through his pockets, taking about fifty dollars. This task completed, they led him back to the safe in the other room and demanded he open it. Instead, Becker grabbed for the first man's revolver, and a struggle ensued.

Graham County deputy sheriff Alexander "Alex" Davis (*middle, with watch chain*). *Arizona Historical Society, PC 161, Ringgold Photo Collection, Box 1, Folder 6, #H.*

While Becker fought with the man with the revolver, the other man began stabbing Becker in the neck and arms, finally driving the blade deep into the clerk's lower back. Astonishingly, Becker broke away from the men, vaulted over the counter and ran out the door to a neighboring saloon, with the knife still protruding from his body. In a panic, the two robbers climbed back out the window through which they had gained entrance, "leaving trail of blood behind, showing one of them had been injured." Becker was in bad shape, having suffered seven knife wounds, two of which were quite serious. Deputy Sheriff Alex Davis was sent for. Dr. William J. Davis, chief surgeon for the Detroit Copper Company, was called in to treat Becker.

After interviewing Becker, Graham County deputy sheriff Alexander "Alex" Davis and Justice of the Peace Albert Brewer ventured to the McCormick store in hopes of finding clues to the identities of Becker's attackers, but it was too dark to properly investigate the crime scene. The following morning, Deputy Davis returned to the store and discovered the blood trail leading away from the mercantile. The officer, in the company of two young "Mexican boys," immediately went in search of the robbers. The thieves had not gone far. The deputy followed the blood trail left behind by the robbers to a house owned by a man named Santiago Contreras, located about one hundred yards from McCormick's store, at the base of a hill.

As the officer and the youths approached the domicile, one of the young boys saw three men, armed with rifles and six-guns, come out of the house. The three suspects proceeded around the far side of the building and began to climb the hill. The boy immediately informed Deputy Davis, who circled around the house until he could see the men. Who fired first is unknown. The initial newspaper reports stated that the lawman fired the first salvo without ever announcing his intentions toward the suspects. Deputy Davis insisted that one of the men turned and fired on him without provocation. The shooting then became general, with Deputy Davis and the suspects firing on each other intermittently, as the latter scurried up the hillside. One of Deputy Davis's bullets found its mark, and one of the fugitives, a tall man in a light coat and hat, crumpled to the ground, wounded. The other two suspects returned to help their comrade up, and the three continued up the hill. Deputy Davis then retreated.

When Deputy Davis first spotted the suspects, he had called on Albert Brewer, who happened to be in the vicinity of Contreras's house, to solicit help from the townspeople. Among those responding was saloonkeeper Pablo Salcido. Although Deputy Davis, who was himself retreating, cautioned against it, telling Salcido to go home and secure a rifle, Salcido recklessly charged straight up the hillside after the fugitives with his revolver in hand. It was then one of the robbers stopped and, resting his Winchester on a rock, took deliberate aim and fired a single shot at Salcido. Pablo Salcido probably never knew what hit him, as the bullet from the rifle pierced his forehead and tore into his brain matter.

By the time Salcido was shot, Deputy Davis was already back down the hill, and the suspects were quickly disappearing over the crest of the hill. What occurred on the other side of the hill is a bit of a mystery and was never fully explained either in the press or at Chacón's trial. The *Guardian* indicated that Deputy Davis and several men from the town circled around the hill and were waiting for the three suspects on the other side as they came down. In the ensuing gun battle, two of the suspects, who were not immediately identified by the newspaper, were killed, and the third man was discovered cowering beneath a bush. He had been wounded in the arm, and the bullet, after going through the appendage, had creased his breast. This man was taken into custody by Deputy Davis. The surviving suspect did not have a weapon in his possession.

The *Graham Guardian* named thirty-nine-year-old Augustine Chacón as the suspect who was wounded by Deputy Davis and noted that he was "believed to be the man who killed Pablo Salcido." An unidentified author in the *Brimstone Gazette* called the Gunfight at Morenci "[t]he most famous gunfight involving the Chacón gang." In fact, it is the only recorded gunfight involving Chacón. As historian and professor Christine Marin pointed out in her biographical sketch of Chacón, "There are no written records to show that Chacón was involved in [any other] criminal activities or that he was legally held responsible or tried in court for [any other] incidents."

Not that it particularly mattered. Chacón's two companions, later identified as Luna Pilar and Leonitas Morales, were dead, and the territorial press and the public wanted someone to pay for taking the life of Pablo Salcido. Chacón was the only one of the suspects still available to answer for the crime. Whether he had actually shot Salcido or not—and as shall be seen, he probably did not—was irrelevant to the case. The fact he had been on the hill at the time of the shooting was enough to have him indicted and, possibly, hanged. From the beginning, the case of *The Territory of Arizona v. Augustine Chacón* was about retribution, not justice.[1]

Origins

Biographical details about Chacón's early life are few. His grave marker states that he was born in 1861, and the *Arizona Republican* suggested he was originally from the state of Chihuahua in Mexico and had relatives in Mimbres, in the New Mexico Territory. However, Graham County historian William Ryder Ridgway indicated that Chacón was born in Arizpe, Sonora. Lios Rios, a resident of early Solomonville, in an interview, remembered Chacón and his brother-in-law visiting Rios's father's ranch in Divisaderos, Sonora, about three hundred kilometers southeast of Nogales, when Rios was still a youth. Chacón is also said to have worked for a time as a peace officer in El Tigre, Sonora, just south of Agua Prieta, "and as a vaquero, who had a penchant for stealing cattle and horses."

Some authors contend that Chacón first arrived in the Arizona Territory as early as 1885, showing up in the town of Tombstone in Cochise County. There are no extant documents or evidence to corroborate these claims,

El Tigre, Sonora, Mexico. *Author's collection.*

outside of some stories of questionable veracity published by the newspapers after he gained notoriety. What can be ascertained with some certainty is that Chacón appeared in the Arizona Territory in either 1888 or 1889 and took up residence in the Safford Valley in Graham County.

It has been alleged that Chacón's first murder occurred during this period. The victim, wrote author Jan Cleere, was rancher Benjamin W. "Ben" Olney, whom Chacón worked for and who refused to pay Chacón the wages due him. In the midst of arguing with Olney, Chacón drew his pistol and shot him to death. When five cowboys came to their employer's aid, Chacón purportedly killed four of them. The fifth cowboy escaped and took word to Olney's uncle, Graham County sheriff George A. Olney. A posse was formed and a manhunt undertaken. Ultimately, Sheriff Olney's posse trapped Chacón in a box canyon. Cleere asserted that rather than surrender, Chacón rode directly toward his pursuers with a revolver in each hand and succeeded in killing four members of the posse.

It is quite a story, and in embellishing it, author R. Michael Wilson declared that Chacón, though gravely wounded in the melee with posse, rode straight for the Olney ranch, where he brutally murdered the remainder of the Olney family, including the sheriff, George. This amounts to more than ten people killed by Chacón in less than a week, which would be pretty impressive feat, were the stories true. Cattleman Ben Olney did reside in Graham County, and his uncle, George Olney, was the sheriff of said county from 1890 to 1894. But there is no evidence that Chacón worked for them, and he certainly did not kill Ben Olney, George Olney or any other members of Olney family. Benjamin W. Olney died on January 20, 1935, in Los Angeles, and George A. Olney died at the age of sixty-six in a New York hospital on April 30, 1927.

This story was the invention of Dan De Lara Hughes, who in 1938 published a highly fictionalized "frontier" biography based on stories his father, Harold "Harry" Hughes, told about living in the Arizona territory in the late nineteenth century. It perfectly exemplifies the persistence of the blatant prevarications about Chacón into the modern era.

Augustine Chacón was said to be well known and well liked among the Hispanic population in Morenci, Solomonville and the other Safford Valley communities, counting Parsomon Enchandia, the young Lios Rios and Sixto Molina among his friends. If, as has often been construed, Chacón was rustling livestock during the period, he must have been quite good at it, as he managed to keep his name out of the newspapers and did not attract the attention of local law enforcement. Only after his arrest in the shooting death of Pablo Salcido did the *Graham Guardian* allude to Chacón having been "wanted for some time by the Sheriff" in connection with various horse thefts, but there was no mention of his involvement in the rustling of livestock prior to this. Then again, Chacón freely admitted that he was a thief. What is in contention are the accusations that he was a murderer.[2]

There persist a few legends about Chacón and encounters he had with John Horton Slaughter, who served as the Cochise County sheriff from 1886 to 1890. The first of these legends will be addressed here, as it purportedly occurred prior to Chacón's appearance in Morenci and the Pablo Salcido affair.

This particular story seems to have originated with author Walter Noble Burns, who in 1927 published a history of Cochise County under the turgid title *Tombstone: An Iliad of the Southwest*. In Burns's wildly imaginative tome, he described Chacón's alleged crimes thus: "Sallying from his stronghold in the Sierra Madres with a troop of desperadoes at his back, this Fra Diavolo of Sonora sacked towns and haciendas, pillaged the stores of merchants, tortured citizens to make them divulge the places their wealth was hidden. He had killed many men and his merciless ferocity had made him the terror of mother Mexico." Burns provided no further details that might make these allegations plausible.

Left: John Horton "Texas John" Slaughter. *Arizona State Library Archives & Public Records, History and Archives Division, Phoenix, #97-7875.*

Below: Cochise County Courthouse, Tombstone, Arizona Territory. *Arizona Historical Society, #9917.*

For some reason, undisclosed by the author, Chacón had "conceived a violent hatred" for Sheriff Slaughter and boasted that he would kill the lawman on sight. This animosity between the desperado and the sheriff "smoldered" for a year or more, until Chacón sent word to Slaughter. Here, in his story, Burns quoted directly from some long-lost missive attributed to Chacón, and conveniently written in English, in which the desperado declared, "I am coming to Tombstone to kill you!" The remainder of the story was allegedly told to Burns by the former deputy sheriff under Slaughter, Albert "Burt" Alvord. This seems highly unlikely, as Alvord had disappeared from the Arizona Territory more than two decades before Burns's book was published.

Alvord purportedly told Burns that he was sitting in the sheriff's office in the Tombstone courthouse when Sheriff Slaughter, whom Burns referred to as "the last knight of Tombstone's Round Table," entered carrying a pair of double-barrel shotguns. He handed one of the weapons off to Alvord, saying, "Come with me!"

Once the two officers were out in the street, the sheriff confided in Alvord, "Chacón is in town! I'm going to get him!"

Slaughter then led Alvord over to "the deep gulch that runs in back of the courthouse along the western edge of town." Beside this arroyo stood "a long house made of canvas stretched over a wooden frame." Although there was no light burning inside, the sheriff assured his deputy, "Chacón is in there." Slaughter then said to Alvord, "You knock at the front door. Chacón will run out the back door." These simple instructions constituted the entirety of Slaughter's plan to capture (or, more likely, kill) "this Mexican bandit."

Deputy Alvord told Burns that he waited until the sheriff had taken up his position near the rear of the structure. "Then, I stepped to the front door, and thumped on it with the butt of my gun." For a moment, all remained silent inside. Suddenly, the report of Slaughter's scattergun "shook the hills." Alvord immediately ran around toward the back door of the structure. When he arrived there, Sheriff Slaughter declared, "I gave him both barrels. He pitched off into the gulch. He must be lying down there dead." As the officers had neglected to bring a lantern, they had to return to the courthouse to procure one. Then they went back to the long house.

"Up and down the ravine we searched," said Alvord, "as carefully as prospectors looking for ore, [b]ut no Chacón could we find, dead or alive." The two officers then returned to the long house up on the bank of the arroyo to investigate further and found "a taut wire that was one of the supports for the tent house." The lawmen reasoned that just as Slaughter fired, Chacón had tripped over the wire and plunged into the arroyo below. "The accident saved his life. The double charge of buckshot had gone over his head. The Mexican had mounted his pony, tied up in the gulch, and escaped."

Burns quoted Alvord as saying, "The situation struck me as funny. But I was solemn as an owl. A sly chuckle just then would have been dangerous. Slaughter had been waiting for a year to kill Chacón, and he was wild with anger at his failure." As the story goes, Chacón skinned out of Tombstone, never to return. Alvord purportedly told Burns, "After it was all over, I went off where no one could see me and had a big laugh all by myself."

Author Allen A. Erwin, in his biography of John Horton Slaughter, included a similar anecdote about a run-in between the legendary Cochise County sheriff and Chacón. In fact, Erwin's anecdote is so similar that one might conclude it was lifted directly from Burns's book and then embellished. This endless reiterating of spurious stories—most of which never appear to have been seriously analyzed or critiqued—appears to have been common practice among these older historians. In perusing the literature previously published about Chacón, one finds the same tales being repeated again and again, without any regard for how factual they might be.

It should not really be necessary to point out the problems with this story. However, given that it continues to be offered up as though it were a credible historical account, it seems a critique is in order.

To begin with, there is the fact that Chacón had no reputation to speak of until after the killing of Salcido in 1895. Chacón was not mentioned by the territorial press at all prior to the Salcido affair, which he most likely would have been had he actually been leading a "troop of desperadoes," sacking "towns and haciendas," pillaging the stores of merchants and torturing and killing citizens. Further, Slaughter's tenure as Cochise County sheriff only lasted from 1886 to 1890, long before Chacón became infamous.

Next, there is the problem of the ongoing feud between Chacón and Slaughter—which has no discernable motive—and the threatening missive. Seriously, who warns anyone in advance of a plan to assassinate them? Additionally, why would Chacón be making his camp inside the city limits of Tombstone, especially so close to the county courthouse, where the sheriff's office was located? Would not a well-known outlaw—a man who, it must be assumed, was on the run—tend to avoid populated areas? Also, how did Slaughter learn that Chacón was in town (it should be noted that Erwin simply glossed over this minor detail)? Did the letter Burns claimed the outlaw sent to Slaughter have a postmark on it? Perhaps a return address? Then, of course, there is the issue of Chacón's horse, which was conveniently saddled and waiting in the arroyo, as though Chacón had planned for the eventuality that he might accidentally trip over a guy-wire and fall into said arroyo. Frankly, the tale is pretty preposterous.

Did Slaughter and Chacón ever meet? It is highly improbable, but what could be better than a titillating story of one of the toughest sheriffs in the history of Cochise County facing off against one of the wiliest banditos of the Southwest? Burns and Erwin prove to be very poor historians but great storytellers, and the publishers of their ridiculous stories probably could not wait to get them into print and sell them to a public clamoring for "authentic," action-packed western tales.[3]

Leaving the tall tales about his time in Tombstone aside, Chacón appears to have been quite industrious during his tenure in Graham County. He would later state that he ran a business in that locale. George Boyd Gamble, a Graham County resident and railroad engineer for the Arizona Copper Company, remembered Chacón as "a mild-mannered, pleasant little Mexican" who worked as a woodchopper and freighter in Clifton. During his trial, Chacón alluded to working with Leonidas Morales at the smelter in Morenci as well. However, it has also been alleged that "he established himself as a leader among a certain clique of Morenci Mexicans, who abetted their meager incomes as miners by occasionally butchering a beef on Bonita Creek or Eagle Creek." The cattle Chacón and his associates were said to have rustled and slaughtered were divided up among the residents in the community or sold to a local butcher shop.

Writer George Leslie Perry—grandson of George Gamble and a friend to Ryder Ridgway—alleged that Chacón had at least one son but did not identify him by name. Perry recalled giving a talk on some of the "renegades" of Arizona—"Black Jack" Christian, the Apache Kid and Augustine Chacón—in Oakland, California. Perry said that there was an older gentleman in the front row at his lecture who became "visibly disturbed and distraught" at the mention of Chacón's name. After the presentation, the man approached the lectern and began to question the speaker extensively about Chacón.

When Perry asked the man why he was so interested "in a stranger who had been dead these many years," the man revealed he was Chacón's son. Perry wrote, "It seems throughout the years, his mother had told him that his father had passed away in Solomonville during an outbreak of smallpox. Through fate, I had to be the instrument to deliver such shocking and hurtful information, and wished a thousand times over that I had chosen some other

Smelter in Morenci, Arizona Territory. *Author's collection.*

unrelated topic, and spared the poor soul such heartache and sorrow." Alas, Perry provided neither the name of the old gentleman nor the name of this man's mother—only the anecdote.

With the exception of Ridgway, very rarely in the many stories circulating about Chacón do any of the writers speak to his family. Of course, he had to have a mother and father and, quite possibly, a son, which would indicate that he also had a wife or lover at some point. In the only verified statement Chacón is known to have made, he stated that he had a family who were "entirely different," but he elaborated no further. Lios Rios, in his remembrance, spoke to Chacón having a brother-in-law, which would indicate that Chacón was indeed married. Ridgway wrote that on April 21, 1980, the Chacón clan gathered in San Jose to erect a monument on his grave. "The catalyst for the event was Charles Venezuela," whom the writer called "a splendid representative of the Chacón family." The author noted that Mr. Venezuela resided in Phoenix but did not reveal the man's relation to Chacón.

Genealogical information regarding Augustine Chacón's family is sorely lacking. About all the information available to the researcher is what was engraved on his gravestone—year of birth, date of death and the name of the cemetery he is interred in. There is no mention of kin—brothers, sisters, uncles, aunts, wives or offspring. Contemporary newspapers reporters never alluded to his family, and his modern so-called biographers and historians have summarily ignored Chacón's ancestors and descendants.

Is this oversight purposeful? Quite possibly. To divest Chacón of a family is, in essence, to divest him of his humanity. As someone's son, someone's brother, someone's uncle, someone's father—a man who loved and was loved—Chacón elicits sympathy and compassion. In short, he becomes a human being, subject to the nobleness and baseness that are inherent to the species. In order to make a monster of Chacón, and make the accusations of heartlessness and savagery against him more believable, it becomes necessary to strip him of his humanity. Removing his familial relations and connections serves to do just this.[4]

What is known about Chacón's life prior to his arrest for the murder of Pablo Salcido is nominal. Not knowing what a legend he would become, no one thought to record anything about his youth or young adulthood, and once he was made famous—or infamous—it did not serve the established narrative to investigate his previous activities or his family history. The evidence that is available—which is almost exclusively concomitant and corollary—indicates that Chacón probably grew up in a rural environment; had little, if any, schooling; and, at best, was only functionally literate. He worked primarily as a manual laborer and sometimes as a vaquero, owned some sort of business (probably supplying wood to the railway) and had no immediate family ties. His criminal activities prior to his arrest in December 1895 were probably limited to rustling and petty theft.

There is nothing whatsoever in the existing historical record that would lead one to conclude that Augustine Chacón was the murderous criminal mastermind and ruthless gang leader the press has come to portray him as.[5]

CHAPTER 2

PUNITIVE JUSTICE

After his arrest, Chacón was taken to Solomonville, the Graham County seat, and incarcerated in the jail at that place, which was located inside the courthouse building. Author Colin Rickards, who wrote for *The West* magazine, stated that Chacón was first taken to Clifton and incarcerated in the rock jail house there before being transferred to Solomonville, but there is no recorded evidence to confirm the truth of this statement.

Solomonville began its existence as a small, predominantly Hispanic community called Pueblo Viejo. According to Anne Freudenthal Solomon—whose husband, Isadore E. "Isaac" Solomon, the town was named for—the settlement originally consisted of "four Mexican shanties...besides our own." However, Isaac had a vision and commenced to make that vision a reality. Having secured a contract to supply mesquite charcoal to the Clifton Mining Company (which was owned by Mrs. Solomon's uncle and cousins), Isaac set up his operation beside the Gila River in Pueblo Viejo.

With the profits he realized from his charcoal manufacturing and freighting operations, Isaac Solomon established a mercantile store, the Montezuma Flour Mill, the Solomon Hotel (operated by Mrs. Solomon) and the Solomonville-Sheldon stage line. Isaac Solomon also served as the first postmaster, after the post office was established in 1878. It was the territorial mail carrier, William Kirkland, who re-christened the burgeoning town "Solomonville."

In 1881, the town of Safford was designated as the county seat in Graham, but in 1882, the courthouse at that place—constructed, like most

The town of Solomonville, Arizona Territory. *Arizona Historical Society, PC 161, Ringgold Photo Collection, Box 2, Folder 20, #A.*

buildings in the area, from adobe block—collapsed after a heavy monsoon rain. Possessing as he did the attendant political influence that comes with the accumulation of wealth, Isaac Solomon was able to have the county seat moved to his town and have the new Graham County Courthouse built there. It was in this courthouse in Solomonville, completed in 1883, that Augustine Chacón would be tried for the murder of Pablo Salcido.[6]

On December 21, 1895, Augustine Chacón was given a preliminary examination before none other than Justice of the Peace Albert Brewer. Justice Brewer ordered Chacón be held over to await the convening of the grand jury. The *Graham Guardian* alleged that Chacón was one of the men who had attempted to rob McCormick's store and stated that he was also wanted by the sheriff for stealing horses from a number of local men and businesses. There was no mention of any murders being attributed to him.[7]

Chacón would spend the next four months languishing in the Graham County jail awaiting his day in court. Finally, during the third full week in April, the grand jury was empaneled and, after reviewing the evidence against him, indicted Chacón (under the name "Augustin Chacón") on two counts of assault with intent to commit murder and one count of burglary. The grand jury was composed completely of white men.

Isadore E. "Isaac" and Anna Freudenthal Solomon. *Arizona State Library Archives & Public Records, History and Archives Division, Phoenix, #97-8471.*

Left: William M. Lovell, Chacón's defense attorney. *Arizona Historical Society, Buehman Photo Collection, #B4058a.*

Right: Associate Justice Owen Thomas Rouse. *Private collection.*

Augustine Chacón was arraigned on April 22, 1896, before Judge Owen T. Rouse, just down the hallway from his cell, in the Graham County Courthouse. The territory was represented by Graham County district attorney Wiley E. Jones, who was assisted by William H. Barnes. As Chacón was without means, the court appointed William M. Lovell to represent him. At Chacón's arraignment, Lovell "informed the court he would soon be called away." The court subsequently appointed attorney James Montague McCollum to assist Lovell in preparing Chacón's defense. The defense team asked for one day before entering a plea. This was granted. The following day, the defense counsel entered a plea of "not guilty of the offense as charge in the indictment." Chacón's trial was set for April 30. Unfortunately for the defendant, when he arrived in court that morning, Judge Rouse continued the trial until Wednesday, May 26.

Justice Owen Thomas Rouse was raised in Missouri and was a graduate of the Union Law School in Cleveland, Ohio. A "Dixie Democrat," Rouse served in the Missouri state senate from 1880 to 1884. When Grover Cleveland won the presidential election of 1884, Rouse requested from him an appointment as a judge in Utah, the New Mexico Territory or the

Arizona Territory. In November 1885, Rouse was appointed U.S. district attorney for the Arizona Territory. In 1889, when Republican Benjamin Harris succeeded Cleveland, Rouse resigned his appointment and went into private practice in Tucson.

Cleveland was again elected to the office of the president in 1892 and, recognizing the former district attorney's loyalty, nominated Rouse as an associate justice for the territory. On April 25, 1893, Rouse was assigned to the Second District, which comprised the counties of Gila, Pinal and Graham. Rouse moved from Tucson to Solomonville and resided there during his four years on the court. During this period, the jurist, as a member of the Territorial Supreme Court, wrote more than two dozen opinions and set two precedents, one of which would have a direct relevance to the case of *The Territory of Arizona v. Augustine Chacón*.[8]

The First Day's Proceedings

Assistant District Attorney William H. Barnes. *Arizona State Library Archives & Public Records, History and Archives Division, Phoenix, #97-6512.*

On the morning of May 26, the trial process began with the selection of the jury that would hear the case. After several potential jurors were dismissed for cause, a special venire was called forth. W. Johns, Herman Hills, P.O. Peterson, R.D. Duncan, Ebenezer P. Bryce, J.H. Sparks, B.F. Gray, A. Leithed, John West, Charles Smith, H.J. Gray and D.V. MacCall—again, all white men—were empaneled to try the case. Judge Rouse then called for a recess until 2:00 p.m. When the court reconvened, the first witness to be called to the stand on behalf of the prosecution was Deputy Sheriff Alex Davis. To Assistant District Attorney Barnes fell the task of questioning the witness.

Deputy Davis was first asked if he knew the defendant. He replied that he did and had known Chacón about five years. "I was pretty well acquainted with him," said the lawman, "would see him going around [Morenci], and then go off and come back." When asked if Chacón knew of Davis's "official character," the deputy answered, "I suppose so." These initial queries led in to the prosecuting attorney asking about the "disturbance" on the night of December 18.

Deputy Davis told of responding to an alleged burglary at Mrs. McCormick's grocery store at about midnight. Before going to the scene of the crime, he had stopped in at Salcido's Saloon to see Paul Becker, the store clerk. Becker told him that somebody had tried to rob the store and murder him. "I asked him if he knew who it was, and he said he did not." Becker then asked if the deputy would pull the knife out of him, as he was not capable of doing it himself and no one else seemed willing to assist with its extraction. "I done it," said the deputy. Deputy Davis took his leave of Becker and, taking the knife with him, ran to the store. When he arrived there, he found the door locked.

Although he never said in his testimony how he was able to gain access, Deputy Davis managed to enter the store. He stated that he lit a candle and "seen blood all over the floor." At same point, Justice of the Peace Albert Brewer joined the deputy in the store. The officer recalled giving the knife to Mr. Brewer, who carelessly left it on the mantel inside the store, whence the knife disappeared, only to be found again on the corpse of Luna Pilar. Deputy Davis, in searching the store, said that he noticed "a little blood on a part of the window where [the suspects] went out the back part of the store. I did not do anything more until morning, when I struck the trail."

Early the following morning, Deputy Davis returned to the crime scene and found a blood trail leading away from the store and up "a very steep hill." He reasoned that one of the suspects had cut his hand, but the court disallowed this part of the testimony. As he ascended the hill, Deputy Davis was joined by "two Mexican boys" and "another young fellow." They "just followed along with me," said Davis. The trail of crimson led directly to the home of Santiago Contreras. When the officer realized that the blood trail continued on into Contreras's house, he said he yelled out to Justice of the Peace Albert Brewer, who happened to be nearby, and told him to go and find some men and bring them.

By his own estimation, Deputy Davis was standing within thirty feet of the house when one of the boys turned to Deputy Davis and said something along the lines of "There goes three armed men." When asked by the prosecutor which direction the three men had proceeded, the witness replied, "They come right out, and went right around up the canyon, going sort of southwest." Attorney Barnes asked Deputy Davis what happened next.

"I ran to the back of the house," said Davis, "and I saw them climbing the hill, and just as I got up on the hill to see this fellow Pilar [Luna], he raised his Winchester and fired at me."

"Where were the other men? Where was Chacón?" inquired Barnes.

"Chacón was behind him."

"How far away?"

"About 10 feet."

The deputy said that Chacón paused in his ascent, turned and fired at him as well but missed. "They were going up the hill; they would go a few feet and the turn around and shoot." Deputy Davis estimated that the suspects fired two or three shots apiece in this manner. By this time, the lawman said, the citizens he had called on Mr. Brewer to assemble were beginning to gather down on the street, including saloonkeeper Pablo Salcido.

"I never seen them until the fight commenced," said Deputy Davis. "When the fight commenced, I shot and emptied my six shooter, and then re-loaded it again. The last time was the time I wounded Chacón. [The suspects] had got over a bunch of rocks by that time. I then started down the hill, and then is where I met [Pablo] Salcido." The saloonkeeper said to the deputy, "Come on, and let us catch these fellows!" To which Deputy Davis replied, "No. Let us get some guns and go around the hill. There is one of them killed or wounded." Summarily ignoring the admonishments of the officer, Salcido proceeded up the hill, with his pistol in hand.

"That was the last I seen of him," said Deputy Davis.

After this interaction with Salcido, Davis stated that he left the hill and went back into town. The next time he saw Chacón, he had been captured. "[Chacón] was sitting down about 35 of 40 feet from where he was first shot. The other fellow [Pilar Luna] was up a little further and he was killed." Leonidas Morales had also been killed. Chacón had been shot in the arm. The prisoner was searched by Deputy Davis and Mr. Walter Bell, but no firearms were found on his person. However, his two companions were found to have three Winchesters and three pistols between them.

The prosecutor asked if Chacón had said anything to the deputy. The witness replied, "He made some remark. I don't know exactly what he did say, He spoke something in Spanish to me. I did not understand him at the time."

Under further questioning, the deputy revealed that the knife he had entrusted to Albert Brewer for safekeeping had been found on the corpse of Pilar Luna. The officer was then shown the light-colored coat that Chacón had been wearing when he was arrested and was asked if recognized the garment. Deputy Davis said he did. "Do you know where on his person your shot took effect; the shot that hit him?" asked the prosecutor.

"I struck him right along in the arm."

"Can you see the place on the coat?"

"That looks like the place," said the deputy, indicating the sleeve of the coat.

During the cross-examination by defense attorney Lovell, the deputy said the firefight between the fugitives and the ad hoc citizens' posse lasted about ten minutes, and "there was pretty regular firing." When asked if he had announced himself to the suspects in his official capacity as a law officer and stated his intentions, he admitted he had not. "I did not have time; they shot the first shots." Deputy Davis stated that Pilar Luna was the first to shoot at him, then Chacón and then "the other fellow."

When asked when Chacón went down, Deputy Davis said Chacón had fallen immediately after he had shot him—"sort of fell over forwards right behind some rocks—up the canyon behind some rocks." Attorney Lovell then asked Deputy Davis if he had seen Salcido get shot. Deputy Davis said, "At the time he was shot? No, sir. He was over the hill from me." In fact, although he stated that Chacón had been firing a Winchester during the melee, Deputy Davis could not conclusively state that it had been Chacón who had shot and killed Salcido, as he had not been present on the hill when the killing occurred.

During the re-direct by the prosecution, attorney Barnes asked Deputy Davis if Chacón had seen him when they first exited the Contreras house. Davis said he had. Upon further questioning, the deputy admitted that Chacón had been trying to escape up the hill and had probably not actually seen the deputy until after Luna fired his first shot. The prosecutor ended by asking if any of the suspects had a cut on their hand when they were examined after the fight. "This man Pilar had his hand cut. Cut across here," said the deputy, indicating the inside of the hand. "His hand was cut across there and was bleeding."

Deputy Davis's testimony confirmed that Chacón had been shot through the arm prior to the killing of Salcido and that, as evidenced by the cut on his hand and the knife found in his possession, Pilar was one of the two burglars who had assaulted Paul Becker the evening before. Deputy Davis also admitted that he had not identified himself as a law officer undertaking to make an arrest and simply assumed that Chacón knew him to be law enforcement at least. Most importantly, Davis had not seen who shot Pablo Salcido.

Justice of the Peace Albert Brewer. *Arizona State Library Archives & Public Records, History and Archives Division, Phoenix, #97-8066.*

Justice of the Peace Albert Brewer was the next to take the stand as a witness for the prosecution. He testified to being present at the saloon that Mr. Becker retreated to immediately after the robbery of the store, as well as to being present in Mr. Becker's rooms at the store while Deputy Davis was conducting his initial investigation of the crime scene. Over the objections of the defense counsel, which called his testimony "immaterial and irrelevant," Brewer described Becker's wounds in some detail and testified that he had "assisted the Doctor in dressing the wounds."

When asked about the knife that Deputy Davis had pulled from the back of Mr. Becker, Mr. Brewer said the officer had given it to him while they were "in Mr. Becker's room" at the store. When asked what he had done with the knife, Brewer said, "I laid it upon the little mantle piece." Brewer stated there were about six other persons in the store at the time, including Santiago Contreras, implying that it was Contreras who took the knife from the mantle and returned it to Pilar Luna. This testimony elicited an objection from the defense attorney, which was overruled by Judge Rouse, and an exception filed.

The prosecuting attorney next asked Brewer about the events of the morning of December 18, 1895. Brewer recalled that at about 9:00 a.m., "Mr. Davis halloed at me from the point on the right hand side of the canyon as you go to Clifton…and said 'Al, come quick and bring help!'" By Brewer's estimation, the deputy was about seventy-five to one hundred yards distant when he hailed him. Brewer admitted that he "did not grasp the situation," and not having a weapon on his person, he just stood and watched as Deputy Davis exchanged shots with the suspects. When the officer came back down the hill and hurried off toward town, Brewer said, "I ran with him."

The prosecution asked Brewer if he had observed Salcido, to which he replied, "I met Salcido with a pistol in his hand going towards these parties that was doing the shooting. Mr. Davis told him he had better get his Winchester." This statement elicited an objection from the defense counsel, which was overruled. Brewer stated, "I did not see Salcido fall back, but I heard that Salcido was shot." Brewer stated that he eventually returned to where Salcido lay and found that he had a single bullet hole in his forehead. He said he believed the shot had come from farther up the hill. "[B]ut from where I stood the hill obstructed my view, and I was not in sight of the man who shot Salcido."

Brewer went on to say that he knew Chacón and recognized him as one of the men who had fled the Contreras house. Mr. Barnes then asked where the bodies of the fugitives had been found in relation to where Salcido lay. Brewer stated that Chacón was nearest to Salcido—about one hundred yards distant. The body of the next outlaw was another one hundred yards up the ravine, and the third was fifty yards beyond that. The prosecution then asked if the witness had much experience with Winchester rifles and, receiving a positive reply, inquired if Brewer believed "the distance from where Salcido was shot to where you found Chacón within shot of a Winchester?" This query brought an immediate objection from the defense, which was summarily overruled. Brewer answered in the affirmative.

In cross-examining the witness, Lovell seemed much more interested in establishing the chain of evidence for the knife used to stab Mr. Becker than in establishing that Brewer had not actually seen who had killed Pablo Salcido. The attorney asked about the style of knife (a sword-point Bowie), the blood on the knife, whether Brewer was certain it was the same knife, where on Luna's body the knife had been found and so on. When Mr. Lovell did finally get around to questioning Brewer about the firefight and the death of Salcido, he neglected to point out that Brewer had not actually seen who shot the man. Instead, the attorney asked how many weapons were found on the dead men?

"3 rifles and 3 six-shooters," answered the witness. "Two of [the rifles] were on a man by the name of named Morales, and he had a six-shooter, and Pilar Luna had two six-shooters and a rifle."

Lovell then asked the witness to state how far the bodies of Morales and Pilar were from Chacón. Brewer said the nearest was about one hundred yards from Chacón's position. "And over a ridge?" asked the attorney.

Brewer did not answer the question directly, saying instead, "If [Salcido] had been standing he would have been in sight of Chacón."

"And Chacón had nothing—no arms?"

"No, Sir."

Obviously, the attorney was attempting, very poorly, to establish that Chacón had been wounded and did not have a firearm on his person with which to shoot Salcido; further, he had no immediate access to a weapon either, as his nearest ally was more than one hundred yards away.

Strangely, Lovell put the following questions to Brewer: "Do you know who burglarized the store? Were you there? Did you see anybody do it? Do you know who stabbed Becker? Did you see it?" When the witness answered no to these questions, Lovell concluded, "You don't really know anything about it?" However, as Lovell had previously pointed out to the court, Augustine Chacón was not being tried for the burglary or the assault on Becker. He was being tried for the murder of Pablo Salcido. These questions may have been designed to discredit the witness, but it would have been more productive to have stayed on the subject of the death of Salcido and the fact that Brewer had not witnessed that.

During the re-direct by the prosecution, Albert Brewer was shown a diagram or map of the locality of the firefight between the suspects and the ad hoc posse of citizens. He was asked if it was accurate. This led to a general discussion between attorney Barnes, attorney Lovell and Judge Rouse about the map and whether it was correct. Lovell objected to the diagram being admitted as evidence, and Judge Rouse concurred, saying, "Let the witness draw his own diagram." In the end, Mr. Barnes ordered Mr. Brewer to "make a map of that locality and come back to the witness stand after awhile."

Mr. Brewer was then dismissed to go draw his map.

Paul Becker was the next witness to be called by the prosecution. The defense objected immediately to the witness, stating that the prosecution had already established that a felony had been committed at the mercantile. The court overruled counsel's objection and allowed the testimony. Becker went on to describe the burglary and his fight with the thieves. His account differed from that which had been reported in the newspapers previously.

Becker stated that he closed the store at about midnight on the eighteenth and stepped out "to get a little fresh air." He said that he returned about half an hour later. "There is a bar-room attached to the store," said Becker, "and just as I passed the bar-room, I was held up…one was armed with a six-shooter in his hand, and the other with a big knife. They told me to stop, and I did." The clerk said he had attempted to disarm both his assailants when they first captured him, but "they were a little too stout" for him. In retaliation, the man with gun had hit Becker in the forehead with the weapon, opening up a nasty gash.

The two thieves then escorted Becker to where the safe was located and demanded he open it. This he refused to do. The men then threatened to kill him. Becker again attempted to disarm the man with the pistol, and a struggle ensued. At this point in Becker's recitation, the defense again objected. In response, Assistant District Attorney Barnes claimed it was necessary to "show the transaction from start to finish," as it would clearly demonstrate "the desperate character of these men." This time the objection was sustained, and Becker was cut short on his testimony.

Becker stated that he broke free of his assailants and retreated to Pablo Salcido's saloon, taking the knife, which had been imbedded deep in the lower left side of his back, with him. "I did not have the strength to pull it out of me."

The prosecution proceeded to ask Becker to describe his assailants in the burglary and how they were attired. Becker said, "There was [*sic*] two men, one of them I can remember as this man Chacón, and the other was a smaller man." Although Becker readily admitted he "did not see him very well," he said the smaller man was wearing a black sateen shirt. Chacón, Becker stated, was dressed in a cheviot coat, white shirt and "slouch, broad-brimmed hat." The larger assailant was also said to have been wearing a handkerchief over his face. When Becker was shown the coat Chacón had been wearing when he was captured, Mr. Becker said, "It looks just like it. Just like the one he had on at the time."

It was Chacón, Becker insisted, who was in possession of the pistol, while the smaller man was wielding the knife. Even though he confessed "there was not much light in the store, only a candle burning," the clerk said he could plainly see the bandit's eyes peering out above his 'kerchief. The prosecution asked if he saw those eyes in the courtroom, and Becker said he was "almost sure" they were the eyes of the defendant. Over the objections of the defense, Becker was next allowed to answer the prosecution's subsequent questions regarding the wounds he sustained in the struggle with his assailants.

When asked by the prosecution if he had seen Chacón since the robbery, Becker said, "They brought him into the room. He was brought into the room after the big shooting."

The defense's numerous objections to Becker's testimony as being "immaterial and irrelevant" to the case were not sustained by the court, and neither was his testimony stricken from the record. This put Mr. Lovell in the position of trying to figure how best to discredit the witness. The defense attorney began by questioning Becker's recall, asking him how he was able to recognize a man he had only seen for a few minutes, in a highly stressful situation and in very low light with 'kerchief hiding most of his visage. Becker replied, "I think this is the man. Yes, sir, I am quite sure."

When pressed on the matter, Becker stated, "When a person sees another once he cannot soon forget him." A moment later, when asked if he had

had seen Chacón prior to the altercation in the store, Becker summarily contradicted his previous statement, saying, "I do not remember." Further, Becker said that he did not recall if the taller man had on overalls or trousers. He also could not remember if the robber had his hat on during the robbery and whether or not it was pulled down low over his eyes. Becker could not even be certain of the color or the height of the crown of the hat. Becker asserted that the taller man was bearded, which Chacón was at the time, but his beard would not have been visible beneath the handkerchief, which was tied about the bottom half of his face. How then did Becker know he wore a beard?

The defense attorney then reiterated the question posed earlier by the prosecution: "You say that the day after the shooting, they brought the defendant to you?"

"Yes, Sir," answered Mr. Becker. "[Graham County sheriff] Arthur Wight, [Deputy Sheriff] Aleck Davis, and Doctor [William J.] Davis, and they asked me if I thought I recognized him. I recognized him. I identified his face. It was the face I had seen in the store that night." Later, when Lovell asked Becker if the man who he had identified as Chacón was "in the same room that the candle was in," Becker replied, "Yes, Sir, when I got jumped right on me—both of them—and caught hold of me and they held the pistol and the knife to my face and made me stop right there, I was afraid—kind of paralyzed me, for awhile anyway."

Modern forensic studies on the reliability of eyewitness testimony have found that when a weapon is presented during a crime, it significantly decreases the ability of the witness "to give an accurate description of the perpetrator of a crime…because of attention to [the] weapon present during that crime." This is referred to as "weapon focus effect." This would account for the reason Mr. Becker could not recall what type of pants the defendant was wearing, whether or not he had a hat on or what the man's partner in the burglary was wearing.

This also raises the question of how Mr. Becker could miss so many details regarding the men's clothing but still manage to identify a pair of eyes peeking out of the space between the brim of a hat and a handkerchief. Again, modern forensics has explanation for this phenomenon. The first is "suggestibility," in which a memory is altered by information gathered from external sources after the event in question, leading to the creation of a distorted or false memory. Although there is no record of what was said by the officers or the witness when Chacón was brought to his room, leading questions such as "This is the man who attacked you, right?" or

"Are these the same dark eyes you saw?" could very easily have altered and distorted Becker's recall.

It is possible that Chacón was the second burglar in the store, but it is also possible he was not. Perhaps Mr. Becker's memories, distorted by the suggestions of others, whether intentional or not, were faulty. Again, Chacón was not on trial for the burglary of McCormick's store, but for the murder of Pablo Salcido. Since, as the defense pointed out, the fact that a felony had been committed was already established, the testimony of Becker was really unnecessary and only had the effect of prejudicing the jury against the defendant.

Dr. William J. Davis, the same man who had treated Paul Becker for his wounds and whose horse Chacón was alleged by the *Graham Guardian* to have stolen, was the next to take the stand. Dr. Davis was asked to describe what he saw on the hill on the day Pablo Salcido was killed. Davis, who heard the reports of the guns, said, "I was in the house at the time, and I ran out to see what was the matter, and I saw the men going up the side of a hill. I saw the shooting, and saw Mr. Salcido fall. I saw this man that shot him." Then, without prompting, Dr. Davis mollified his statement, saying, "I suppose they shot at him. I saw two men shoot at the time he fell."

In answering the further queries from the prosecutor, whose case his testimony was supposed to be buttressing, Davis's statements became all the more uncertain. Davis stated that he saw only two men shooting when Salcido fell, and he did not see the third of the fugitives. One of the shooters, said the witness, was running up the hill when Salcido was shot, and the other was taking cover in a "little gulch." When asked how far apart the men were, Dr. Davis replied, "I don't know that, I never thought about that." In contradiction of his statement made just moments before, Dr. Davis said that he observed *all three* of the fugitives shooting in Salcido's direction, and he saw Salcido shooting back with his pistol. When asked directly about whether he had seen Chacón shooting, Dr. Davis affirmed that he had seen Chacón. The defense attorney objected, saying the question was "leading." The objection was overruled.

When queried as to which way the defendant appeared to be shooting, Davis said he was "shooting down the canyon towards where Mr. Salcido was standing." When asked how far the defendant was from Salcido, Davis said he was 150 feet or more, directly contradicting his earlier statement about not having paid any attention to the distance between the men. Finally, the prosecution asked him directly whether he had seen Salcido fall, to which he replied, "I did." Davis was then asked, "Who shot the shot just before he fell?" Dr. Davis, again contradicting his earlier statement, stated emphatically, "Chacón."

The doctor was subsequently asked about Salcido's wound. He replied, "I found a bullet wound that entered about the center of the forehead and just went through the lower part of the head, and came out at the base of the brain, a little on the left side."

"Was that wound fatal?"

"Yes, Sir, I should think it was."

Prosecutor Barnes then asked the witness to describe what Chacón had been wearing on the day of the shooting, Dr. Davis stated the defendant was wearing "a light-colored hat—a sombrero" and a "light-colored coat." The coat, he said, was "covered in blood," ostensibly from his wound. Dr. Davis identified the two pieces of clothing that had been admitted into evidence as the same hat and coat he had seen the defendant wearing on the day in question. When asked what Luna and Morales were wearing, the doctor replied, "One of them had on a black coat, and he had on blue overalls, and the other had on a blue jumper and blue overalls."

Prosecutor Barnes then asked whether Salcido was alive or dead when the doctor reached him. "He was dead," replied Davis.

When defense attorney Lovell, during his cross-examination, called into question the vantage point from which Davis observed the firefight, Davis revealed he had been standing "about 400 yards away" on the porch of Bud McLain's house and admitted that Salcido had been standing between him and the three men, facing away. The attorney then asked how many shots were fired before Salcido went down, how many shots were fired immediately afterward and whether, in fact, the shooting was "a continuous fusillade of shots fired from either side?"

The witness stated there had been a lull in the shooting when Salcido fell.

"You don't know whether the man you thought was Chacón fired at Salcido?" asked Lovell.

"I could not swear he fired at him," came the reply from the witness.

"Were there not a good many men shooting at the same time?"

"At that very moment?"

"Yes, sir."

"I don't think so: I could not swear there were."

Dr. Davis's testimony became even more convoluted and confused when the attorney began asking him if he had seen Deputy Davis wound Chacón. At first, he stated he had not seen Chacón get shot. When asked if he saw Deputy Davis during the fight, the witness said he had, but the deputy was not shooting. In his next statement, Dr. Davis contradicted himself once more.

"You did not see [Deputy Davis] until he was there shooting?" asked the attorney.

"Yes, sir."

"Where was he when you saw him?"

"He was going with someone, up the mountain in pursuit of Chacón."

Seemingly exasperated, the attorney asked, "Did you see him after he quit shooting and before Salcido was shot? Where was Davis when Salcido was shot?"

"I don't know. I didn't see him," came Dr. Davis's disaffirming reply.

Attorney Lovell subsequently asked Dr. Davis if he had not actually "judged the kind and color" of the clothing the men on the hill were wearing after the fight was over—in retrospect. The doctor replied in the affirmative, although he insisted that he had been able to distinguish between the man with the black coat and the man with the light coat as they were "going up the hill 400 yards away."

The defense attorney questioned him on a few other points and then finally put the question to him directly: "Do you know who shot Salcido?"

"No, sir, I do not."

Mr. Barnes, in a re-direct, attempted to salvage the credibility of his witness, asking leading questions about which way Chacón seemed to be pointing his rifle (all of which were objected to by the defense). Lovell countered, asking the witness, almost rhetorically, "And you say that 400 yards away that you could tell that this defendant was pointing his gun at Salcido?" Dr. Davis replied, "I do not. I say it only appeared to me. I may be mistaken."

There were a few more questions from the prosecution, but Lovell had very successfully called into question the reliability of Dr. Davis as an eyewitness, or so it would seem.

Regino Chavarria followed Dr. William J. Davis on the witness stand. As English was not Chavarria's native tongue, a translator named Pedro Michelena was brought in.

In answer to the prosecuting attorney's inquiries, Chavarria stated unequivocally that he had been about eighty yards from Pablo Salcido when the latter was felled by the bullet. Chavarria stated that he had seen Chacón forty to fifty yards farther up the hill. The prosecution asked pointedly if the witness had heard a shot from a gun before Salcido went down. This brought an objection from the defense that was overruled; an exception was

Pedro Michelena, who served at the translator at Chacón's trial, stands in the back. *Arizona Historical Society, PC 161, Ringgold Photo Collection, Box 1, Folder 6, #H.*

taken. In answer to this query, Chavarria asserted that he had heard the shot and that it had come from the rifle in the hands of the defendant.

The defense objected to the prosecutor's original query as being "a little suggestive." The question was rephrased, and the witness's answer changed.

"In whose hands was the gun just at the time the shot was fired?"

"I saw the gun laid on top of a rock," replied Chavarria, through the interpreter.

"And who was behind the rock, holding the gun, if you know?"

"Augustin Chacón, judging from the head."

The defense attorney moved this answer be stricken from the record as well, but Judge Rouse overruled the motion. Again, exception was taken by the defense.

Under further questioning, Chavarria confessed that "a big rock obstructed the view; I could only see the hat and face." The prosecutor asked if the witness had seen Chacón near the rock prior to the shooting. This question was objected to as being "leading," and the objection was sustained.

"Had you seen Chacón a few minutes before this shot, and if so where?"

"No, sir."

"Had you seen Chacón on the hillside there before that shot, and if so where had you seen him?" (Objected to. Objection overruled. Exception taken.)

"Yes, sir."

"How near to that rock had you seen him last?"

"Just behind the rock."

"Did you see him just before he got behind the rock?"

"Yes, sir, I saw him when he went around the rock."

"How long was that before the shot?"

"8 or 10 minutes."

Chavarria continued answering the prosecutor's questions and identified the hat and coat, which had been entered into evidence, as being the same Chacón had been wearing on the day of the murder. At this juncture, the prosecutor left off with his examination of the witness.

The first question Lovell asked of Chavarria during cross-examination was whether he was involved in the fight.

"Yes, sir."

Lovell then asked, "How many shots did you fire?"

"Not a one."

"Then you were not in the fight?"

"Perhaps."

"Did you have a gun?"

"No, sir."

"What were you doing out there?"

"Looking on."

Under further questioning, Chavarria's story continued to change. Initially, he had said he was eighty yards from Salcido, but under cross-examination, this distance became thirty yards. When asked about his vantage point by the prosecutor, Chavarria stated, "I was inside of the house, right close to where this took place." When asked the same question by the defense attorney, Chavarria first stated, "I was in the house."

"Did the door face towards where the fight was going on?" asked Lovell.

"Yes, sir, I was outside, I was not inside."

"Were you behind [the house]?"

"Yes, sir."

Chavarria further claimed that he had seen Deputy Davis wound Chacón, but in direct confutation of the lawman's sworn testimony, Chavarria alleged that Chacón had not fallen down when he was struck by the bullet. He asserted that Chacón crawled up toward the big rock when he was wounded, and this was five or six minutes before Salcido was shot. When the question of the amount of time between Chacón being wounded and Salcido being killed was put to him a second time, Chavarria contradicted his testimony again, saying it had only been "two or three minutes—just a moment."

When asked if he saw Chacón after the shooting of Salcido, Chavarria said he did not know what became of him. He also stated he did not know how Chacón came to be unarmed or what happened to the Winchester with which he was alleged to have killed Salcido. "I don't know anything about that," he said.

Under further questioning by the defense attorney, Chavarria's story changed once again. He stated that although Salcido had a six-shooter in his hand, he did not actually see him shooting at anyone. When asked how it was that he saw Chacón and Salcido at the same time, the witness replied, "When the report of the gun that wounded Salcido was fired, I heard Mrs. Salcido scream, and I ran to where Salcido fell." Mrs. Salcido was standing at the kitchen door, and it was her scream that attracted his attention. "Standing at the kitchen door, they saw him fall."

"After Pablo fell," said Chavarria, "I started in the direction where he fell, and I saw a gun pointed in the direction where he fell, and I heard screams below, and I started up to where…"

The attorney interrupted here, saying to Chavarria, "You saw a gun pointed over the rock, and you did not know but what they was [*sic*] going to take a shot at you?"

"Yes, sir."

"And you did not know that Salcido was shot until you heard the family cry?"

Chavarria replied, "No, sir, I saw him fall, and I heard the shot fired, but I still saw the gun pointed in that direction, and I fell back, and when I saw the family in the condition they were I ran up to where Salcido was, and I picked him up and he was dead—he was then dying."

When questioned as to what kind of gun he saw sticking up over the rock, Chavarria could not state with certainty if it was a shotgun, a Winchester or a large pistol—only that it was a "long gun."

From the scaffold, Chacón would call Regino Chavarria a liar, saying, "A good many people are in the habit of saying a good many things that are not true, as Mr. Chavaria [*sic*] did." This assertion on Chacón's part regarding Chavarria's deceitfulness may well have been founded in fact. Certainly, Chavarria's testimony was confused and contradictory, with his story continually changing as more questions were put to him. By way of example, at first, he stated unequivocally he had seen Chacón with a rifle in his hands and saw him shoot Salcido. However, as Chavarria was further interrogated, he admitted that he only saw the rifle sticking up over the boulder and only the hat and eyes of the man behind it. Later, Chavarria confessed that he was not even paying attention to what was going on up on the hill until he heard Mrs. Salcido scream, which one would assume she did *after* seeing her husband killed.

Chavarria's entire testimony was filled with such inconsistencies, which would lead one to conclude that he had not seen all he claimed to have seen. The question is: Why would this witness be compelled to lie? At this remove, it may never be ascertained why Chavarria fabricated a good portion of his testimony. What is known is that he earned for himself the enduring ire of Chacón, who named Regino Chavarria as one of his sworn enemies.

After Chavarria stepped down, Faustian Candelaria took his place in the witness box and was duly sworn in. Again, the interpreter was Pedro Michelena. Under oath, Candelaria stated that he was at home and was about one hundred yards from Salcido when he went down. When asked who shot Salcido, the witness replied, "All I know is that the last man who reached that rock went around it, and the shot was fired, and after the shot was fired, I saw him stand up, and it was Chacón." He stated that the defendant was wearing a white hat. Conversely, he stated that Chacón's coat was dark.

During the cross-examination, Mr. Lovell asked Mr. Candelaria pointedly, "Now, isn't it a fact that all you knew about Chacón—how he was dressed—was after you saw him, after he was shot and wounded, and then you saw he had on a light hat, and that coat, isn't that all you know about it?" The witness replied, saying that he had seen Chacón "going up the hill" and that "he turned his face toward me." When asked if Chacón was wearing a beard, Candelaria answered, "Yes, sir, I could not tell whether it was a beard or not, I saw his face was black as an indication of a beard."

Under further questioning, Candelaria again altered his testimony, claiming that he knew it was Chacón who fired the shot. "He faced me when he went around the rock and got behind it." The defense attorney next asked if he had seen Deputy Davis wound Chacón, to which the witness applied in the affirmative. "Isn't it a fact that Chacón kept on going, and went clear up on the mountain side after that shot was fired by Davis?" asked the attorney. "Yes, sir," came the reply. Candelaria elaborated, saying that Chacón was not running up the hill but rather "traveling at a long walk" as he was wounded on the left side.

"Isn't it a fact that when Davis shot Chacón and wounded him that the two men that were with him took his gun and went over the hill?"

"No, sir, when Davis wounded Chacón, they helped Chacón up, and kept on traveling."

"Didn't one of the parties take Chacón's gun with him and went over the hill."

"No, sir, I did not see it if he did."

"What became of Chacón's gun, if he had one?" asked the attorney.

"I don't know, but the gun could be seen."

When asked again if the man behind the rock was in plain view of the witness, he replied, "No, I could not [see him], but as soon as he fired the shot he stood up and I could see him." When asked where Chacón's confederates were at the time, Candelaria stated they were farther up the hill. When asked if they were firing their weapons as well, Candelaria answered, "I did not see them whether they did or not." When pressed on the subject, he said, "I could not see them because the hill stopped the view of them."

This ended Candelaria's testimony, which, unlike Chavarria's, was beneficial to the case of the prosecution. Candelaria swore that he had seen the shot fired, and subsequently the man who fired it, and that man was Chacón. However, the witness stated the man behind the rock was wearing a dark coat, which contradicted the testimony of all of the previous witnesses as well as the physical evidence that had been admitted. This seemingly minor detail would take on more significance when the defense witnesses took the stand. Also, Candelaria could not explain how Chacón came to lose his rifle, even though he claimed to have been watching all three of the suspects as they ascended the hill.

After Candelaria vacated the witness's box, Albert Brewer, the justice of the peace, was recalled on behalf of the territory to exhibit his hand-drawn map. The prosecution asked that Brewer's hand-drawn map be entered into evidence. The defense agreed on the condition the map be accompanied by the witness's explanation, as well as that it could be subject to cross-examination. This stipulation was allowed by the court, and Brewer showed his map to the jury, explaining the legend. The first question from Lovell was about the scale of the map. When Brewer gave vague estimates concerning distances, Lovell changed his mind about the map being entered into evidence. The court sustained his motion to have it excluded, and the map was withdrawn. Albert Brewer then stepped down.

Mrs. Pablo Salcido was the next to occupy the witness box. The widow was first questioned by Assistant District Attorney Barnes. In answer to the queries of the prosecutor, Mrs. Salcido stated that she had seen her husband fall from the vantage point of their home, forty to fifty yards distant. She said she had seen a person standing behind a rock near the top of the hill. Under further questioning, the widow Salcido stated that she saw the top of a hat behind the rock but made no mention of seeing a gun. She did say that she thought she had heard the shot that took the life of her husband and that it had come from directly in front of him.

Mr. Lovell began his cross-examination but was only able to ask a single question before Judge Rouse called for a recess for the evening. The court was adjourned until the following morning, Wednesday, May 27, at 9:00 a.m. The jury was "admonished by the Court according to the law," and Chacón was removed by the sheriff's deputies to his cell on the far side of the building, next door to the sheriff's office.

The Second Day's Proceedings

The first to take the stand on Wednesday morning, after the court was called into session, was not Mrs. Salcido, but Albert Brewer, who was recalled by Assistant District Attorney Barnes. Barnes attempted to clarify the distance between Deputy Davis and the three suspects, as well as who fired the first shot. In reply, Brewer said that the lawman "was at a point about 50 yards from me, about half way between me and where the three men were." When asked how far the men were from the house when the first shot was fired, Brewer estimated "a little less than 100 yards."

"Who fired the first shot?" asked Barnes.

"One of these three men."

"It was not Davis?"

"No, Sir."

During the cross-examination of Brewer by the defense, when asked which of the three men—Chacón, Morales and Luna—was in front when the firefight began, Brewer stated, "I could not see them because the last few steps that I took in the direction I was running placed me just out of sight of these men; there is a little draw there that just hid me from their sight." Still, Brewer insisted that the first shot of the melee had been fired by the suspects, but he could not ascertain which one of them had fired it.

Albert Brewer was the final witness to be called by the prosecution.

In opening the case for the defense, Mr. Lovell moved that "all testimony as to the alleged burglary and the alleged assault on the witness Becker" be stricken from the record. The motion was sustained, with Judge Rouse admonishing the jury, "[E]xcept for the purpose of showing that an offense had been committed…the assault on Becker will not be considered." The prosecution filed an exception.

The first witness to be called by the defense was Walter L. Bell, a resident of Morenci for "about eight years," who professed he had seen Salcido shot. Bell stated that while there was a lot of shooting going on, there had been a brief lull in the gunfire, and this was when he heard the shot that took the life of the saloon owner. Bell further stated that this particular shot had come from "a little canyon above Salcido, from over a rock." He went on to explain that he saw man going up the hill, although he was unable to provide a positive identification of the man. This unknown man, Bell recalled, "turned around suddenly and pulled his gun down, and fired, and Salcido fell back dead. It seemed it was done in an instant."

The defense attorney then asked the witness to explain what occurred after the firefight ended. Bell said he had seen Pablo Salcido's body about a half hour after he was shot. He also saw Chacón "sitting under a bush on the hill." He reported that the defendant "was in great pain, apparently wounded. I pulled his clothes to see where he was hurt. It looked as if he had been shot in his breast. He said his arm was shot, but I did not see that at the time." Bell said that he searched Chacón for weapons "but did not find anything." When asked again about Chacón's condition at the time he saw him, Bell replied, "He apparently [was] in great agony; he said he was badly hurt."

Bell stated that a guard was left with Chacón, and he proceeded up the hill with the other officers to view the bodies of Morales and Luna. Pilar Luna, the witness said, was about one hundred yards up the hill from where Chacón was apprehended. He was dead. The body of Morales was farther up the hill, about sixty or seventy-five yards distant, "right up on the divide." When asked if Morales had any weapons on him, Bell replied in a manner that did not directly answer the query or was even in context, saying, "He was there when we got there, his clothes were burning."

When queried by the defense attorney as to where he was in relation to Salcido when the latter was shot, the witness replied, "I was standing directly across the canyon, right on the line."

"Did you have a full view?"

"Yes, Sir."

The cross-examination of Walter Bell by the prosecutor was brief, with Barnes asking him if Chacón was one of the men he saw going up the hill, if he was wearing a coat and if all three were armed. Bell stated that he did not recognize Chacón as one of the men, although he might have been. He said that he had not noticed what the suspects were wearing but that, yes, they had all been armed. "How far was Chacón from the place where that shot was fired that killed Salcido?" asked Lovett. "He might have been 60 or 75 yards up the hill, sitting under a bush," came the witness's reply.

Bell had not provided much new information with his testimony, but he had attested to the fact that Chacón did not have a weapon on his person when he was discovered sitting, wounded, beneath the bush and was taken into custody. This was significant, for how could a man with no weapon have killed Salcido?

Ms. Alice Pratt took Walter Bell's place on the witness stand and was sworn. When asked where she resided, Ms. Pratt stated that she "had a room in the saloon of Jose Colimo in Morenci" and was residing at that place on the day Salcido was killed. She said she was in bed when the shooting commenced and "got up and sat in the door and saw the rest of it." She went on to say that she had seen Pablo Salcido get shot and had distinctly seen the man who shot him. "How was the man dressed who fired the shot that killed Salcido," asked the defense attorney.

"He was dressed in dark clothes—very dark."

"Did you see one of them dressed in light clothes?"

"Yes sir, one was dressed in light and two in dark."

"Did the one dressed in light have on a light hat?"

"I believe he did."

"And the man that did the shooting you say was dressed in dark?"

"Yes sir."

"Where was the man that was dressed in light clothes with the light hat when the shot was fired that killed Salcido, by the man that was dressed in dark clothes."

"He had disappeared over the hill before Pablo Salcido was shot—went over the ridge; over the top of the hill from my view."

During the cross-examination, the prosecutor first tried baiting the witness, asking, "You say that you did not see the shot fired, but you saw the man just after?" Ms. Pratt corrected the attorney, saying, "I saw the shot, the gun was through a bush." The prosecutor then asked. "Or over a rock?" to which the witness replied, "There is a rock *and* a bush there." Ms. Pratt admitted that she did not see the man in dark clothes until after the shot was fired, when he stood up, but insisted that he was the only one on that side of the hill, his companions having crossed over the ridge on to the other side, out of her line of sight.

The attorney then attempted to attack Ms. Pratt's credibility. He asked if she had not engaged in separate conversations on Christmas Day with a Mr. Jones and a Mr. Smith, also known as "Musical Smith," and if she had not told Jones and Smith that it was man wearing a light hat and light clothes who shot Salcido. Ms. Platt vehemently denied that she had told either of these men such a thing.

"Swear you did not?" asked Barnes.

"No, Sir!"

Ms. Pratt's testimony was the most important presented by the defense up to this point. She was steadfast in her description of the man who had killed Salcido—insisting that the man was wearing dark clothing, not light—and she was not dissuaded from her testimony by the machinations of the prosecutor. Despite this, Ms. Pratt was not the defense counsel's ace in the hole.

After her bellicose exchange with the prosecuting attorney, Ms. Pratt was allowed to step down, and Concepción Castro took the stand in her place. As Castro was not fluent in English, Pedro Michelena was called on to interpret. The witness attested to the fact that he had been asleep in his rooms on the upper floor of Dominic Sartoris's saloon when he was awakened by the sound of gunfire. Castro stated that he went into the hallway to watch the drama unfold on the hill and that he plainly saw Chacón when he was shot by Deputy Davis. Moments later, he saw Morales and Luna pulling the wounded Chacón up the hill, "then Pilar turned around and fired the shot on Salcido."

"How was Pilar dressed that fired the shot on Salcido?"

"Dark—dressed in a dark suit."

During his examination by the defense attorney, Castro stated that his vantage point was higher, and he had to look down from where he was to see the fight. However, under cross-examination, he confessed that although his rooms overlooked Salcido's house, the saloon was not on top of the hill but rather down in a canyon—in fact, he had to look *upward* to see what was going on the hill. "[The saloon] was lower," said Castro, "but you can see very well from there." Unfortunately, by calling into question his vantage point and causing him to change his story in this regard, the prosecutor had essentially discredited him as a reliable witness. Still, Concepción Castro had identified Pilar Luna, who was dressed in dark colors, as the killer of Pablo Salcido, which was in perfect agreement with the testimony of Ms. Pratt.

The next witness to be sworn in on behalf of the defense was Paz Vialobos, who also required the aid of the interpreter. He stated that he was also residing upstairs in Sartoris's saloon in Morenci on the day Salcido was killed and knew both Chacón and Pilar Luna. When asked directly whether he had seen the man who shot Salcido, Vialobos unhesitatingly replied, "Yes sir."

"How was the man dressed that shot him?"

"He wore a black shirt, and a bluish looking coat—dark looking coat."

"Do you know who that was?"

"Pilar." The witness went on to say that Chacón was "a short distance away" from Luna and Morales, sitting down.

Mr. Barnes, during the subsequent cross-examination, asked if, when the shot was fired, the three suspects were close together. Vialobos replied in the negative. When asked if he had seen Luna and Morales helping Chacón up the hill after he had been wounded, he said he had. The witness said that this occurred prior to Salcido being shot, and it was only after the three men had separated that he heard the shot fired. "But they all had guns, didn't they?" asked the prosecutor. "Yes, sir," answered Vialobos, "I cannot tell how many. They all had guns, and the gun that Salcido was killed with was a Winchester."

"All of them were shooting?"

"Yes, sir, they were all firing, but after they wounded Chacón, they did not fire any more."

"You say after Chacón was shot, he fired no more?"

"No."

Vialobos remained adamant that it was Pilar Luna, not Chacón, who had shot and killed Salcido. When the prosecutor asked if the witness had known Luna, he freely admitted he had. When asked if he knew Chacón, he said, "No, I am not very well acquainted." He said he did not know Morales at all. "Did you see [Luna and Morales] after the fight?" asked Assistant District Attorney Barnes.

"Yes, sir." Vialobos elaborated on this answer, stating that he had gone up to the top of the hill that very afternoon to view the bodies of the two men.

"Were not these men buried up there on the hill where they were killed?" asked Barnes. This question met with an immediate objection from the defense attorney, which was overruled and an exception taken.

"Yes, sir," came the answer.

"Did you put candles up there for several days after they were killed?" asked Barnes.

"No, sir." This question was also objected to by the defense, and it was asked it be stricken from the record. The objection was sustained, and Paz Vialobos was dismissed.

The combined testimonies of Ms. Pratt, Mr. Castro and Mr. Vialobos should have been sufficient to raise substantial doubt in the minds of the jurors as to who had actually fired the shot that killed Salcido. In point of fact, only two of the prosecution witnesses, Chavarria and Candelaria, had identified Chacón as the gunman (and Chavarria, as evidenced by the number of times he contradicted himself and changed his story, was most likely lying), while three of the defense witnesses stated emphatically that it was man clad in dark clothing—most probably Pilar Luna—who had done the killing. The next defense witness would also identify Luna as the killer, and this witness was actually on the hill when Salcido was killed.

Augustine Chacón was the last to be called to the witness box. He was duly sworn in by the clerk of the court. Pablo Michelena again performed his duty as the interpreter. Chacón gave his name and identified himself as "the defendant in the case now upon trial." When questioned about the burglary of McCormick's store, Chacón said that he knew Mr. Becker and knew where the store was located, but he insisted that he had not been inside the store "or on any part of the premises on the night before the shooting of Salcido." Further, the defendant declared that he knew nothing "about anybody being in that store or saloon, and cutting Mr. Becker that night."

Chacón was asked if he had known Pilar Luna and Leonidas Morales, to which he replied he had. "I knew Morales there working in the smelter." The defendant was then asked if he had been wounded in the firefight on the day Salcido was killed. "Yes, sir, I was," came the reply. When pressed for details, Chacón stated, "I was climbing on top of a rock when I was wounded in the arm [and] a flesh wound creased me on the breast." When asked about the subsequent actions of Pilar and Morales, Chacón replied, "They were just a little ahead of me, and the moment they saw I had been wounded, they came and helped me."

The defense attorney subsequently changed subjects, inquiring specifically about Pablo Salcido and whether Chacón had seen him that day. Chacón said that he had not. When asked if he knew the deceased, Chacón stated he had known him "about seven years" and that their relation was "friendly." The defense attorney then asked if the defendant could say where he was when Salcido was shot. This brought an objection from the prosecution, which was sustained by Judge Rouse. The defense attorney re-directed, asking, "Do you know whether or not, after you were wounded, did you fire a shot."

"No, sir," answered Chacón, "I did not have a rifle."

"What became of your weapons after you were shot, if you had any?"

"They were taken from me."

"Who took them away from you?"

"Leonidas."

Mr. Lovell then instructed Chacón, "After they were taken away from you state whether or not you rested on the hill." This provoked an objection from the prosecution as being leading. Judge Rouse told the defendant, "State what you did."

"I remained there in that spot," said Chacón.

The defendant was then asked if, after his weapon was taken from him, his confederates had fired any more shots. Chacón answered, "From my own knowledge, Pilar fired one," and immediately afterward, "he spoke to Leonidas, who was near by [*sic*], and stated, 'Come right up, I have already killed one.'" When asked what he was doing while this interaction was occurring, Chacón replied, "I was lying on my side, because I could not do otherwise." When asked why he could not do otherwise, the defendant said, "It pained me all over, and I was throwing some blood too."

Asked if he knew Deputy Sheriff Davis, Chacón said he knew Davis and had seen him as "I was climbing up, going up the hill." Lovell asked, "Did Mr. Davis say anything to you?"

"No, not a word." Mr. Lovell ended the direct examination at this point, and the cross-examination commenced.

The first question put to Chacón by the assistant district attorney was, "You were running up the hill from Davis at the time, were you not?"

"I was going up the hill," was the reply.

"And Davis was behind you?"

"Yes, sir."

The next question, "Did you know he was a constable or Deputy Sheriff?" raised an objection from the defense attorney, which was overruled by the court and an exception taken. "Yes, sir," was the terse reply of the defendant.

The question immediately after, as to whether Chacón had been in Contreras's house immediately before his flight up the hill, brought another objection from the defense counsel, "as not cross-examination." This objection was sustained, and the question was withdrawn by the prosecutor.

Mr. Barnes abruptly changed the topic, asking if Chacón had been at Becker's store the night before the shooting. Chacón replied in the negative. Barnes then asked where Chacón had slept that night. Lovell objected, saying, "I did not ask where he slept." The objection was overruled, and exception taken. Chacón answered, "I slept in the house I went out of… Santiago." When asked what time he had arrived there, Chacón stated that it was "between one and two," presumably in the morning.

"Who went with you?" asked Barnes. Lovell objected.

"Who went there in the house with you?" Lovell objected again, and the objection was sustained.

Barnes seemed to leave off with this line of questioning in order to pursue another: "Where were you when you first saw Davis that morning?"

Chacón answered, "There in the house."

Then the prosecutor tried again to provoke an answer from Chacón regarding who had been in the house with him, asking pointedly, "Who else was in there when you saw him." Lovell objected to the question as being immaterial and irrelevant, and the objection was sustained by Judge Rouse. Barnes returned to the subject of Davis's appearance at the home of Contreras, asking where the lawman was when Chacón first noticed him.

"He was standing at the corner of the house," replied the defendant.

"Did you come out of the house as soon as you saw Davis?"

"I saw him after I went out."

"Did you see him before you went out?"

"No, sir."

"What did you go out for?" This question prompted yet another objection from the defense attorney, which was overruled by the judge, and an exception taken.

"Because I heard noise of the others going out, and I followed them," said Chacón in reply to the query.

"Did you take a gun with you?"

"Objection!" countered Lovell. "Objection overruled!" replied Judge Rouse.

"Exception!" said Lovell. Chacón answered in the affirmative.

"Did the other men have guns?" asked Barnes.

"Yes, sir…Pilar had a Winchester .44, and a six-shooter .44."

"And what did you have?"

"A Winchester. I had a .40-60 Winchester."

"What did the other man have?" asked Barnes. Again Lovell objected, as the question was "not cross-examination." This objection was sustained. Barnes asked Chacón for a second time if he had come out of the house as soon as he saw Deputy Davis. "I saw him after I came out," was the defendant's rebuttal. The assistant district attorney then asked if Pilar had

had a knife on his person, eliciting another objection from Lovell, which was sustained.

"What was you running away from Davis for?"

"Objected to as not cross-examination!"

"Objection overruled," said Judge Rouse, "but that question is not proper in form."

Barnes reworded the question: "Why were you running away from Davis?" This brought another objection from Lovell, which was sustained by the court.

At this point, the prosecutor left off with the questioning of the defendant, and Chacón was allowed to step down. Chacón being its last witness, the defense team rested its case. If there were closing arguments by the respective attorneys, they were not recorded in the official transcript of the trial.

That afternoon, May 27, 1896, Judge Rouse orally gave instructions to the jury on behalf of the Territory of Arizona. The defendant, through his attorney, also filed a set of instructions to the jury, but three of these—Nos. 3, 7 and 9—were refused by the court. The first of these, No. 3, stated that if Deputy Davis had not identified himself as a law officer, Chacón had the absolute right to defend himself against the officer and his ad hoc posse "and to repel [illegible] by force, and to resort to the use of a deadly weapon if necessary to save his own life," and Chacón should therefore be acquitted.

The second of these instructions, No. 7, stated, "If a person is killed by a bullet fired from a pistol or a gun, and two or more persons each at the same time fire loaded pistols or guns at him, and one of the persons who fires is on trial for murder, and there is no evidence of a conspiracy between the parties who fired, and the jury are in doubt as to which shot killed the deceased, the defendant on trial is entitled to the benefit of that doubt, and he should be acquitted."

The third of these instructions, No. 9, stated "[I]f the jury are unable from the evidence, to determine by which of said persons (Chacón, Morales, or Linas) the shot was fired. Then the jury should consider the case precisely the same as though it had been proved that some person other than the defendant fired the fatal shot."[9]

After the two sets of instructions were read, the jury was sequestered to deliberate the case. The *Graham Guardian* opined, "The prosecution made out an exceedingly strong case, and a verdict of guilty of murder was confidently expected."

The newspaper was correct in its prediction. It took only two hours for the jury to return to the courtroom. The foreman, R.D. Duncan, read the verdict: "We the jury, duly impaneled and sworn in the above entitled cause, upon our oaths do find the defendant guilty of murder as charged in the indictment. We the jury ask the mercy of the Court in favor of the defendant." The jury was then discharged, and Augustine Chacón was "remanded to the custody of the sheriff until the further order of this court.

Five days later, on Monday, June 1, 1896, at 10:00 a.m., Chacón, and his attorneys—Mr. McCollum, Mr. Patterson and Mr. Lovell—were again standing before Judge Rouse. Also present was Graham County district attorney Wiley E. Jones. The judge explained to Chacón that he had been given a "fair and impartial trial in this Court" and had been found guilty of murder "as charged in the indictment." Judge Rouse, through the interpreter, Mr. Michelena, asked the defendant if there any reason the sentence should not be pronounced.

Chacón replied, "I have nothing to say except that I am not guilty of the crime which I am charged."

Judge Rouse subsequently sentenced Augustine Chacón, ordering the defendant be "kept in close confinement [by the Graham County sheriff] until the 24th day of July, A.D. 1896, when, you Augustin [*sic*] Chacón, shall be, by said sheriff, taken to some private and convenient place within this said Graham County, and be by said sheriff, between the hours of 10 o'clock A.M. and 3 o'clock P.M. of said 24th day of July A.D. 1896, hanged by the neck until you are dead. And may the Lord have mercy on your soul."[10]

CHAPTER 3

A FUTILE APPEAL

Moments after sentence had been pronounced on his client, Chacón's attorney James McCollum filed a motion for a new trial on the following grounds:

1. That the court erred in admitting in evidence the testimony of the witnesses Paul Becker, Albert Brewer, Aleck Davis, and others as to the specific detail and account of the alleged burglary of the store in charge of the witness Becker, and the assault upon and cutting and stabbing of the witness Becker on the night previous to the homicide or murder for which the defendant was upon trial in this cause, over the objection of defendant.

2. The court erred in giving each and all of the instructions which were given and asked for by the Territory.

3. The court erred in refusing to give instructions numbered 3, 7, and 9 asked for by the defense.

4. The verdict of the jury is contrary to the law and the evidence.

5. The verdict of the jury was and is contrary to the evidence and not supported thereby.

The Pima County Jail was located in the Pima County Courthouse. *Arizona Historical Society, Buehman Photo Collection, Places-Tucson-Buildings-Pima County Courthouse (second), #B205699.*

Judge Rouse, "after hearing the grounds for said motion and the argument by counsel thereon, and being fully advised in the premises," flatly overruled and denied the motion. There would be no second trial for Augustine Chacón in the Graham County District Court. However, Mr. McCollum was not to be dissuaded so easily and immediately filed an exception to Rouse's ruling "and gave notice of an appeal from said ruling and decision to the Supreme Court of the Territory of Arizona." The following day, the attorney filed his Notice of Appeal with the court and was given thirty days' time to file a Bill of Exceptions and Statement of Facts.[11]

The day after the Notice of Appeal was filed, Chacón was moved from the Graham County Jail in Solomonville to the Pima County Jail in Tucson.

Juan Chavez (alleged name) and Augustine Chacón at the Pima County Jail. *Arizona Historical Society, PC 1000, Main Photo Collection, Portraits—Chacón, Augustine, #29909.*

The reason for the move, said the *Arizona Daily Star*, "was not so much the insecurity of the jail there, as the fear that Chacón's friends would attempt a rescue, which, in fact, they had threatened." The origin for this rumor was not disclosed by the newspaper. The *Arizona Weekly Citizen* reported on July 25, the day after Chacón had been scheduled to be hanged, that his execution had been postponed indefinitely. "Stipulations have been filed in the case granting the lawyers until September 1st to perfect their appeal."

The most famous photograph of Augustine Chacón was taken during his incarceration at the Pima County facility. The man standing beside him has never been conclusively identified. In the photograph, Chacón seems to tower over his companion, even though Chacón was reported to be only five feet, nine inches in height. This explains why so many later authors, who never bothered to investigate further, stated that Chacón stood over six feet tall.[12]

Said appeal was duly submitted on the first day of June 1896, and notice was given by the defense counsel to the district court of the Second Judicial District, staying the execution of sentence. On July 31, the *Graham County Bulletin* noted, "Chacón is now in the Pima county jail for safe keeping, where he will probably remain until he knows his fate from the supreme court."

Six months later, Chacón's case was brought before the Supreme Court in Phoenix. On Sunday, January 10, 1897, the *Arizona Republican* announced the convening of the court the following day, saying, "The calendar is not a very long one, but it embraces several important cases." These included "[t]he cases of two members under sentence of death, Augustine Chacón, Graham county, and [Sergeant] Philip Lashley," who murdered Private John Sanders at Fort Huachuca.

In its society column, the newspaper noted, Judge Rouse had been in Tucson the previous Monday. "He goes from there to Phoenix, where the regular term of the Territorial Supreme Court begins." At the time, there were four justices on the Supreme Court, all of whom were Southern Democrats—Albert Cornelius Baker, the chief justice; Joseph D. Bethune, associate justice; John Jay Hawking, associate justice; and Owen Rouse, associate justice. Justices Baker and Bethune had fought for the Confederacy, and in defense of the institution of slavery, during the Civil War. Rouse, of course, was Chacón's trial judge in the district court. Today, it would be expected that judges would recuse themselves from a case because of a potential conflict of interest or lack of impartiality. However, during this era, justices often heard appeals of cases that they had heard in the lower courts.

Chief Justice Albert Cornelius Baker. *Arizona State Library Archives & Public Records, History and Archives Division, Phoenix, #97-6490.*

We do not know if Judge Rouse heard Augustine Chacón's appeal, as almost all of the documents in the case appear to have been lost. The Bill of Exceptions and Statement of Facts prepared by the defense attorneys have long since disappeared. Also missing are the arguments of counsel before the court. What remains available to the researcher in regards to the Chacón appeal are the original complaint and indictment, the notice of appeal and some other miscellaneous documents from the first trial.[13]

The *Republican* recorded on January 14 that "[t]he attention of the Supreme Court was confined to Graham county litigation yesterday. The case of Augustin Chacón, appellant, under sentence of death, was argued and submitted." The newspaper went on to briefly recount the stories of the burglary and the shooting death of Salcido and review the legal grounds for the appeal. Somewhat prematurely, the *Graham Guardian* reported on January 22 that "the supreme court sustained the findings of the district court in the Cachon [*sic*] case."

The reason, during the trial, why Judge Rouse had felt confident in cherry-picking the defense counsel's instructions to the jury for what he believed was appropriate to present was that he himself had set a precedent that allowed him to do so. In the 1894 appeal to the Supreme Court of the territory in the case of *The United States v. Chung Song*, in his opinion in this case, and citing Penal Code 1887, paragraph 1677, Rouse wrote (emphasis added), "Either party in a criminal action may ask that special instructions be given [the jury]. The court must endorse upon each instruction the word 'Given' or 'Refused,' and under said word the judge must sign his name, etc. The court, in addition to the special instructions above mentioned, may charge the jury, stating to them all such matters of law *as it may think necessary* for their information in giving the verdict."

In other words, by this opinion, which he authored, Judge Rouse had guaranteed that he was perfectly within his lawful right as the trial judge in refusing to give the jury the entire set of instructions requested by the defense counsel, while providing to the jury the complete set of instructions requested by the prosecution in the case.[14]

The Supreme Court recessed soon after hearing the appeal in the case of the *Territory v. Chacón* and, according to the *Arizona Republican*, was out until Tuesday, February 23. The reason for this long adjournment, which commenced on January 16, was not disclosed. On the morning the court reconvened, nineteen decisions were handed down, including a decision in Chacón's case. "The case of Agustin Chacón vs. the territory, Graham county, was affirmed," reported the newspaper. "The appellant is lying in jail at Tucson under the sentence of death, the date of which has passed. Upon a return of the remitter, the court below will direct a warrant re-setting the date of execution."

Among the court documents extant, the only primary source document relating to the actual appeal is a single handwritten paper, authored J.B.L. Alexander, the clerk of the Supreme Court. It is dated from February 18, 1897, and reads as follows:

> *In Supreme Court, Territory of Arizona, January Term, 1897*
> *Augustin Chacón*
> *Appellant*
> *Territory of Arizona*
> *Respondent*
>
> *This cause having been heretofore argued by counsel for appellant and respondent respectively and submitted, and the Court having taken the same under consideration, and the Court having fully considered the same and being fully advised in the premises, It* [sic] *is ordered that the judgement of the lower Court herein be and the same is hereby affirmed.*
>
> *Supreme Court*
> *Territory of Arizona…*
>
> *In witness thereof, I have hereunto set my hand and affixed the official seal of said Supreme Court this 18th day of March, 1897, at Phoenix, the Capital of Arizona.*
>
> *J.L.B. Alexander (signed)*
> *Clerk.*[15]

Alas, this is all the information regarding the appeal of Augustine Chacón that remains.

Graham County deputy sheriff John C. Epley (*seated, third from the left*). *Arizona Historical Society, PC 161, Ringgold Photo Collection, Box 1, Folder 6, #H.*

The *Daily Star* reported on April 23, 1897, that Deputy Sheriff John C. Epley of Solomonville and another officer had arrived in Tucson the previous day for the purpose of escorting Chacón back to Graham County. It was later reported in the *Graham Guardian* that as the prisoner was being returned to Solomonville, the officers discovered that his shackles had been sawed in two. Chacón allegedly told the officers that "he did that before being taken to Tucson." When he finally arrived in Solomonville, new leg irons were fastened on the prisoner.

Under the headline "Sentenced to Hang," the *Graham County Bulletin* reported on the afternoon of April 24 that Judge Rouse had re-sentenced Chacón to be hanged and set his date for execution as June 18, 1897. The newspaper went on to provide its readers with a highly inaccurate retelling of the break-in at McCormick's store—increasing the number of burglars to four and having Becker almost "stabbed to death" in the melee—as well as of the gunfight on the hill. In the *Bulletin*'s version, Pablo Salcido was not rushing up the hill madly with a pistol in hand, but approaching demurely with the intent of petitioning the men surrender. This change in Salcido's role in the drama, from reckless posse man to benign peacekeeper, would be disseminated by later authors, including Jennie Parks Ringgold, Joseph Miller and Harold Edwards, into the modern era.[16]

Since his return to Solomonville, Chacón was said to have "talked freely with his guards" and was quoted as saying that "he had never seen anything yet he was afraid of, but had never tackled the gallows before." The newspaper further reported that when he had been brought into court for his re-sentencing, "the courtroom was well filled, and many of the people were standing on their feet to get a glimpse of Chacón's face, but if they were expecting him to show any signs of emotion, they were badly disappointed." Chacón was said to have stood there stoically "and slowly stroked his black moustache and bowed in assent."

"Chacón, the noted outlaw and slayer of Pablo Salcido is to be hung [*sic*] June 18th," stated the reporter for the *Bulletin*, who then asked, rhetorically, "Will there be no one to feel a pang of pitty [*sic*] or sorrow at his death[?]"

Conversely, Judge Rouse, who sentenced Chacón, wrote to Governor Benjamin Joseph Franklin to say that when he imposed the sentence of death originally, he felt it fit the crime. "Since then he is of the opinion that the sentence was too harsh, but when the case came back, affirmed from the supreme court, he was unable to mitigate the punishment in resentencing him." Rouse laid the blame on the Nineteenth Legislative Assembly, which in 1897 had redefined homicide and the punishment thereof. The act also repealed all the previous and prior laws regarding homicide in the penal code. On May 2, while re-sentencing Chacón, Judge Rouse "stated from the bench that it was his opinion that no proceedings could be had for homicide under an indictment found previous to the law passed by the Nineteenth Legislature, other than for murder in the second degree."

In fact, this change to the penal code should have saved Chacón's life, as his attorney would later assert. The Nineteenth Territorial Legislature, commonly referred to as the "Tin Horn Legislature," had assembled in January 1897. Among the eighty-eight laws passed was "an act which repealed the three sections of the penal code of Arizona that defined homicide and substituted a new definition." The issue was with the final two sections, which read:

> *Sec. 4. Paragraph 276, (Section 276), 277 (Section 277), 278 (Section 228) of Title III, Chapter 1, Entitled "Of Crimes against the Person," of the Penal Code of Arizona are hereby repealed.*
>
> *Sec. 5. This Act shall take effect and be in force from after its passage.*

The *Arizona Republican* explained the immediate effect of the bill thus: "In order to supersede a law by a similar one, the first is wiped out of existence at the instance the other is created. When the old law of murder was repealed the crimes of the defendants under it ceased to be crimes. The new law could not be made applicable to acts committed before its passage for then they would be ex post facto laws, and unconstitutional." By not including a caveat in the bill, such as "[s]ave and except as to such cases as may be now pending," it basically "repealed all penalties for murder (except that prescribed for manslaughter) which were committed prior to the enactment of the new bill; the effect of which will be that no law exists for the punishment of murder committed prior to the meeting of the last legislature."

The *San Francisco Call* had a field day with the new law, deriding it as "defective." The newspaper stated, "The new law repealed the old law, but failed to provide for the cases then pending," as in the case of Augustine Chacón. "[N]ow the best lawyers in the Territory cannot agree as to whether Chacón and the other seven murderers can be convicted of murder in the second degree or only of manslaughter." In an update to the initial story, the *Call* noted that this oversight would affect at least fifteen cases in the territory. As to Chacón's case, it was stated, "Although tried and convicted once under the law as it stood before the legislature met, the best legal minds in the Territory are now of the opinion he cannot be legally executed."

For several other defendants awaiting trial in the territorial courts or in the course of having their cases appealed, this oversight in the law was fortuitous. In the case of *The Territory v. John Hawks*, he was acquitted, after his attorneys "argued that under [the law's] construction no person charged with murder committed prior to the passage of the act could be convicted except of manslaughter." Richard Cross, who had brutally murdered Jerome barkeeper Byron Jones in a jealous rage, also benefited from the so-called Norton Act. Cross could not be indicted for anything but manslaughter by the grand jury, to which he pleaded guilty. "Judge [John J.] Hawkins did the best he could under the law and gave Cross the maximum sentence, ten years."

In a situation very similar to Chacón's, William Schultz, who had been sentenced to hang for the murder of W.K. "Old Man" McNary in 1895, had appealed his case and was granted a new trial. "While the case was pending," reported the *Arizona Sentinel*, "the 'Tin-horn' nineteenth passed a law making it impossible to convict him of the crime for which he had been sentenced to hang." Schultz was found guilty of manslaughter and given ten years in the Territorial Prison in Yuma. When the Cochise County

Grand Jury appealed to District Attorney Allen English for clarification, English referred them to Associate Justice Joseph D. Bethune, who "instructed that in cases of murder committed prior to the enactment of the criminal law referred to, indictment for manslaughter only could be found."[17]

Cochise County district attorney Allen R. English. *Arizona Historical Society, PC 1000, Main Photo Collection, Portraits—English, Allen R. #7156.*

In the case of *The Territory v. Augustine Chacón*, the new law should have applied. The *Arizona Republican* reported that among the papers submitted to the governor in its petition for clemency was "a letter from Judge Lovell to Judge McCollum in which, after eluding to the numerous errors in the lower court, he expressed the opinion that in view of the homicide law enacted by the late legislature, Chacón could not have been legally sentenced, although he has been tried and convicted before the old law was repealed."

Echoing these sentiments, McCollum included the following missive among the documents to be sent to the governor in the defense's request for executive clemency:

> *The Territory of Arizona*
> *vs.*
> *Augustine Chacón*
>
> *Comes now the defendant Augustine Chacón, and moves the Court to suspend the sentence of death on the judgement of death heretofore rendered in this action for the following reasons, to wit:*
>
> *That since said judgment was rendered and prior to this date, to wit: on the 16th day of March, 1897, the Legislative Assembly of Arizona Territory repealed the law of Homicide, and especially that part of said law providing for punishment thereof by imposing the sentence of death, and that there is not now any law authorizing the court to pronounce any other sentence upon him greater than imprisonment in the territorial prison for a period of ten years.*
>
> *J.M. McCollum*
> *Attorney for the Defendant*

District Attorney Wiley Jones countered, writing to the governor to describe "the difficulty encountered [in Graham County] in the punishment of crime," specifically those described as "bloody and red-handed murders," and how Chacón was the first perpetrator who "had been brought so near the gallows." The fact that the evidence presented at the trial did not conclusively prove that Chacón had killed Pablo Salcido (but actually suggested otherwise), or the fact the change in the territorial statute effectively disallowed the court to sentence Chacón to death, did not seem to concern District Attorney Jones. His only interest was in having Chacón executed—and, by doing so, sending a message to all the other malefactors in his county.

Wiley, it seems, was representing a minority opinion. The *Arizona Republican* reported that the petition that was sent to the governor on Chacón's behalf was "supported by a half dozen members of the jury," who had petitioned the court for mercy in sentencing. "If they believed it would not be heeded," revealed the newspaper, "they would not have found Chacón guilty of murder." One jury member, who signed the petition for executive clemency, in a startling admission, asserted that while Chacón was keeping company with some "desperate characters" and had been on the hill when Salcido was shot, "he did not believe that Chacón fired the shot that killed him."

Still, the *Republican* predicted, "Graham County will have a hanging on June 18th."[18]

The first rumor of Chacón's bloodthirstiness began to circulate while he was still in jail in Solomonville awaiting his execution. A man identified only as Norton, who had spent ten days in lockup with Chacón, was going about Phoenix telling anyone who would listen that Chacón had murdered a fellow inmate by cutting his throat with a razor. The rumor was stolidly dispelled by the *Arizona Republican* on May 23, 1897: "There is no truth in the report at all....Chacón is very peaceable and so far the jailors have had no trouble with him in anyway." Yet as time went by, the tales of Chacón's murderous appetites would only grow taller, and the *Arizona Republican*, which twice defended him, would soon join with the other territorial newspapers in promoting the image of the man as a merciless villain with an insatiable thirst for the blood of his fellow man.[19]

CHAPTER 4

A DARING ESCAPE AND A NASCENT LEGEND

At this point, Chacón had but one chance to avoid the gallows: a pardon from the governor of the Arizona Territory. On June 8, 1897, Chacón's attorney John M. McCollum presented Governor Benjamin Joseph Franklin—another dyed-in-the-wool "Dixie Democrat" who had fought with the Confederacy in the Civil War—with a petition, "signed by many influential citizens of Graham County, among them several members of the jury, which found Chacón guilty," to commute Chacón's death sentence to life imprisonment.

At the interview, "Mr. McCollum made a strong appeal for clemency, and asked the prisoner's sentence be commuted to imprisonment," reported the *Arizona Republican*. "Governor Franklin, after hearing the argument and reading the testimony in the case as given in the district court of Mohave [*sic*] and then the proceedings before the Supreme Court, in which the judgement of the lower court had been sustained," steadfastly refused to sign the petition. "[U]nless a new governor takes his seat before the 18th of the month or providence interferes, the prisoner will expiate his crime on the gallows."

Attorney McCollum was not to be dissuaded and stated that he would apply to Justice Joseph D. Bethume for a writ of habeas corpus, "which would be denied…but the denial would offer a base upon which an appeal to the supreme court of the United States might be constructed."[20]

Augustine Chacón must have decided that the habeas corpus ploy was much too thin and "did for himself what the governor refused to do." On

Territorial Governor Benjamin Joseph Franklin. *Private collection.*

the night of Wednesday, June 9, after he was informed of the governor's decision to let him swing, Chacón broke out of the Solomonville jail. This was accomplished by "sawing through the double layer of two-inch lumber lining the cell in which he was kept, then by digging through the heavy adobe wall into the Sheriff's office, with a small iron bar," while the guards, Joe Reaves and George Burkner, reportedly slept. The saw and the bar were, in all likelihood, smuggled to Chacón by friends on the outside, "but there is no clue…as to who aided him." His escape was not discovered until the following morning, when trustee Peter Monahan entered the sheriff's office to sweep.

"The wall through which Chacón made his escape," reported the *Graham County Bulletin*, "consists of ten inches adobe, lined on the inside with a double layer of two inch pine boards, spiked together with five inch spikes." The newspaper further informed its readers that "Mr. Reaves was sleeping in the empty cell at the west end of the jail and Mr. Burkner was sleeping in the little office opposite the cell occupied by Chacón." The editor observed that cutting a hole through the two layers of pine boards, pulling out the five-inch spikes and digging out the adobe, "necessarily would make considerable noise."

"[S]ome lady relatives" paid Chacón a visit the day before his escape, "with whom he was allowed to converse considerable time," reported the *Bulletin*. "It has been known ever since Chacón was convicted that he had friends who would render him any assistance in their power; last fall it was rumored that his friends would make an attempt to rescue him from the jail, and Chacón was removed to the Tucson jail for safety, where he remained until last month." The newspaper further chastised the county officials, saying, "This should have caused extra precautions to have been taken in guarding him."

The two guards, Reaves and Burkner, were taken to task, in a most sardonic manner, by the *Republican*. "It appears that the supervisors of Graham County, fully cognizant of the insecurity of the jail, had employed three guards at a salary of $75 a month apiece. The supervisors expected them to

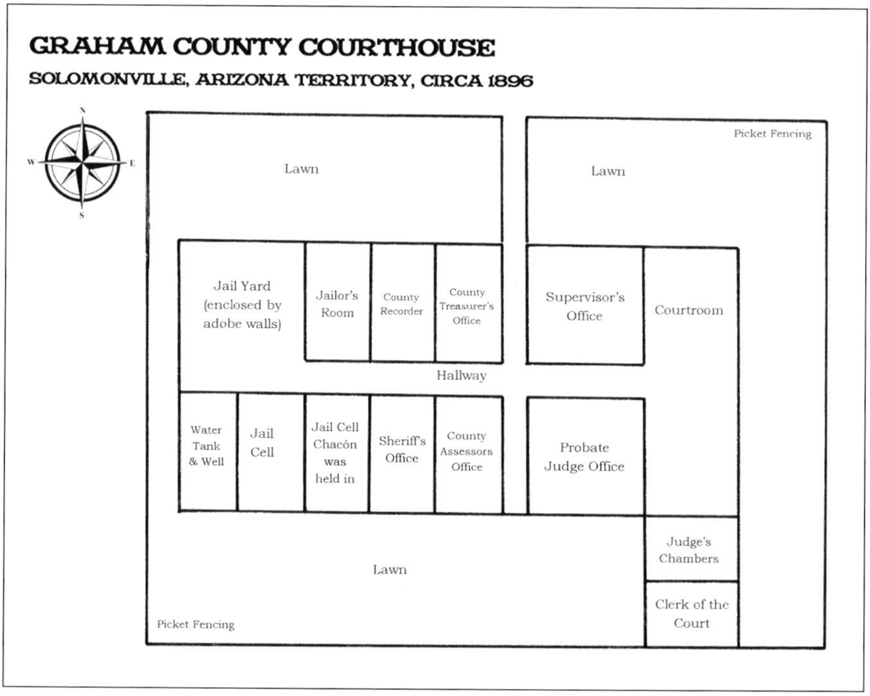

Interior of Graham County Courthouse. *Author's illustration.*

watch, but as no specific contract had been drawn up, the guards imagined that they were hired to sleep." Editor Charles C. Randolph continued on in this vein, saying, "These guards not only gave the county a fair, honest sleep, but introduced novelties in the way of snore, for which no extra charge was made to the county."

The editors of the *Arizona Silver Belt*, Arron H. Hackney and Joseph H. Hamill, were less amused, charging Reaves and Burkner with "gross carelessness" and wondering, editorially, how the two slumbering officers had not been awakened by the noise that Chacón, who was heavily manacled, must have made "sawing through a double layer of two-inch pine boards which lined the adobe wall and which were spiked together with five-inch spikes." Still, the *Silver Belt* editors stopped short of asking for the guards' immediate dismissal.

With his tongue firmly planted in his cheek, the editor of the *Republican* observed, "Whoever may be to blame for the escape, Chacón certainly was not....It is said there is a sentiment in Graham county amounting almost to a religious fervor against hanging...Chacón, in deferment to the sentiment of the community on the subject of capital punishment, and probably holding antagonistic views himself, naturally took his departure, having been informed that the governor meant to do nothing for him." Editor Randolph further noted that Chacón's escape foiled his attorney's plan to submit a writ of habeas corpus on his behalf. "For what is the use of a habeas corpus when the corpus is roaming about, nobody knows where or whither?"

Perhaps the most amusing anecdote by a modern author in regards to Chacón's escape was penned by the eminent storyteller Marshall Trimble in his book *Arizoniana*. As Trimble told it, Chacón was assisted in his escape by "a beautiful senorita groupie" who smuggled Chacón "a hacksaw blade in the binding of a huge family Bible." Over the next few evenings, while the other prisoners played guitar and sang "lusty corridos" to keep the jailers from hearing, Chacón sawed his way through the bars of his cell. On the night of his escape, the "beautiful senorita groupie" returned and, using her feminine wiles, lured the jailer into the backroom. While *la señorita bonita* and *los músicos aficionados* performed their respective roles, Augustine Chacón sawed out the last bar in his cell and escaped from the repressive confines of the Solomonville jail into the night. One must admit that although it has no historical validity whatsoever, Trimble's is a wonderfully imaginative story.

On the evening of the escape, Sheriff William Birchfield and Undersheriff Ben Olney (the same man authors Jan Cleere and R. Michael Wilson intimated was shot to death by Chacón in 1890) were out of town, but they were summoned back via telegram. The local officers were said to have "no clue which direction he had taken," but it was assumed that Chacón would attempt to cross the international border, thereby putting himself beyond the reaches of the territorial authorities. "The chances are many to one that Chacón will never be retaken," opined the *Republican*. "He is a Chihuahua Mexican, as most of the Mexicans about Clifton and Morenci are."

Upon hearing the news that Chacón had given the officers the slip, District Attorney Wiley Jones quipped, "[H]e was gone beyond redemption, perhaps even beyond the limits of Graham county." Paradoxically, his escape would raise Chacón's status in the estimation of the territorial press (and with law enforcement), from that of a common criminal to an outlaw of repute, in the same class as desperados like "Curly Bill" Brocius, "Black Jack" Christian and Geronimo Miranda.

The *Graham County Bulletin* simply stated what was becoming quite apparent when, on June 13, it observed, "Augustin Chacón, the escaped murderer, has been gone nine days, and the posses that have gone out in all directions have returned empty handed and Chacón is probably safe in Mexico by this time." His trail had been picked up right outside the jail and was followed by jailor George Burkner and W.T. Richards "as far as the Detroit Company's pump, but was lost at that point, and never found again." Wrote the editor, "[I]t seems that after Chacón dug through the jail into the sheriff's office, the earth must have opened and swallowed him completely."

The *Bulletin* also provide the most comprehensive description of Chacón of all the newspapers that reported the escape:

> *His weight is about 160 pounds. Height about 5 feet 8 inches. Thick heavy shoulders; good form; stands erect. He wore when he escaped gray woolen pants, blue woolen shirt, no suspenders, gray canvass* [sic] *shoes tipped with tan or russet colored leather.*
>
> *Mustache short and thick, but very little beard; eyebrows heavy, prominent and lowering, covering small, black, piercing, restless eyes. Nose straight. As he has sympathizers likely to aid him, he may have changed clothes since his escape. He gives his age at 41 years, which is about correct. He has coal black hair, with a few gray hairs making an appearance; hair heavy, thick, and long on top; parts hair almost in the middle.*

The newspaper predicted that Chacón would not be captured anytime in the near future, "but he will be heard of again in this county and may yet grace a gallows' stand."

The rewards for his capture offered by Governor Myron H. McCord (who succeeded Franklin on July 29, 1897) and the Graham County Board of Supervisors aggregated to $700, and circulars were ordered sent out to the territorial newspapers and law enforcement officers. The *Republican* doubted that these officials would ever regret offering such an exorbitant amount for Chacón's apprehension, as "the chances are a thousand to one that they will now have to be paid.…A reward is often sufficient to induce Americans to denounce friends for the sake of getting it. For one reason or another, Mexicans are not so readily induced to betrayal. Perhaps it is because they care less for money that their neighbors do."

Still, posses were formed, manhunts undertaken, clues run down and sightings investigated, but to no avail. "Word comes from Solomonville that no trace has been obtained of Chacón," reported the *Republican*. "What is more discouraging, none is expected to be obtained." The editor of the *Florence Tribune*, Charles D. Reppy, made light of the situation (and revealed his anti-Semitic predilection), saying (emphasis added), "Owing to the absence of the principle, Senor Don Augustine Chacón, from *Sheenyville* the other day, the necktie social was unavoidably postponed to a future date, not yet announced. And thus *The Bulletin* lost a society item."[21]

The escape of Chacón made headlines across the country, with the news being disseminated by the Associated Press via telegraph. It was reported with varying degrees of accuracy by the *San Francisco Call*, the *St. Louis Post-Dispatch*, the *Cedar Rapids Evening Gazette*, the *Leavenworth Times*, the *Wichita Beacon*, the *Los Angeles Times*, the *Salt Lake Herald*, the *Fort Wayne Journal-Gazette* (which reported that Chacón had killed Paul Becker, not Pablo Salcido), the *New York Sun*, the *Deadwood Evening Independent*, the *Beatrice Daily Express* (Nebraska) and many more. The item included in the *El Paso Times* on June 11, 1897, which epitomized most of the others aforementioned, read simply:

> *Solomonville, Ariz., June 10—Augustine Chacón, convicted here last fall for the murder of Pablo Salcido in December, 1895, and sentenced him to hang June 18th, escaped from jail here last night. Some one on the outside provided him with a saw, with which he cut through the jail wall into the sheriff's office, which was untenanted.*

Four days after Chacón's escape, Dolph Wilson and John Stewart were riding along Gila River, north of Safford, when they saw a man they thought might be the fugitive. The man was sitting on the riverbank and seemed to be preparing to take a bath. The young men said that "they rode close up and spoke to him several times," but he did not acknowledge them. Suspicioned by the man's actions and his "white skin," Wilson and Stewart rode off out of sight, tied up their horses and returned furtively on foot in order to further observe the man. They stated that "they got a good look at him" and noticed he was armed.

After watching the man for some time, the two youths slipped away, mounted their horses and rode into town to report what they had seen. A posse of armed men was hastily assembled, and the young men led them back out to the place where they had encountered the suspect. However, by the time they reached the spot beside the river, the man had disappeared, and a search of the area turned up nothing. "On Monday, when a picture of [Chacón] was shown to the boys, they said it was the picture of the man they saw." The *Guardian* concluded the item, saying, "No further trace of the man they saw has since been discovered."

It was not long after Chacón's escape that the various depredations being committed in the southern portion of the territory began being attributed to him. The fugitive had only been free eighteen days when it was reported that

Opposite: Augustine Chacón at the Graham County Jail at Solomonville, Arizona Territory. *Arizona Historical Society, PC 161, Ringgold Photo Collection, Box 1, Folder 5, #1.*

Above: The town of Safford, Arizona Territory. *Author's collection.*

"a party of three Mexicans," purportedly led by Chacón, liberated three horses from ranches on the Gila River in New Mexico. W.A. Gilespie, a local rancher, formed a posse to pursue the rustlers, "but, concluding that Chacón was one of the gang, the trail was abandoned, the pursuing party not being prepared for a desperate battle." The *Republican* reprinted and further embellished this report, saying, "When Chacón was arrested, he was at the head of a gang of horsethieves [*sic*], and it is believed that he will not be long in gathering his pals together again."[22]

On Friday, September 10, under the headline, "A Desperate Fight," the *Graham Guardian* reported that Undersheriff Ben W. Olney had killed a "bad Mexican" near the Groesback Hotel, on the outskirts of Safford. Manuel Borgus, who was said to be wanted in the New Mexico Territory for horse theft, had been arrested in town by Olney and was being escorted to the jail on horseback. Suddenly, Borgus grabbed his revolver from the officer and, wheeling his horse about, made a dash for freedom. A running fight ensued, with Olney being joined in the pursuit by several local townsmen.

The chase came to an abrupt end when Borgus's horse spooked, reared and dashed him to the ground. "The Mexican" (as Manuel Borgus was referred to throughout the *Guardian*'s narrative) was on his feet in a moment and sought refuge in a corn patch. With pursuers nearly on him, Borgus deserted the corn patch and dodged behind a nearby house, firing several shots at the officers as he ran. Onley and his men quickly surrounded the building and began closing in on the suspect from either side. One of them called on Borgus to surrender. When he did not, Undersheriff Olney came around the corner of the house and shot Borgus with his Winchester, "the ball entering the right side and passing through the body." Borgus died within minutes.

The *Graham Guardian* proclaimed Borgus "a desperate character" and alleged that he "was close friend of Chacón." Manuel Borgus had the dubious distinction of being the first of Chacón's alleged "friends" to have a run-in with the law. He would not be the last. Over the next five years, any person of Hispanic heritage who committed a major crime in the Arizona Territory would be somehow, in some way, connected to Chacón.

In August 1897, the decomposing corpse of John Miller was discovered, buried in a shallow grave, "in a secluded spot on Eagle Creek, six miles distant from Morenci." In December 1895, the same month McCormick's store was burglarized, Mr. Miller went out prospecting along Gold Gulch, taking along his Winchester for protection. He never returned. "Diligent search was made for Miller by his friends and the officers of Morenci and Clifton, but no trace of him could be found." The search for the missing man was finally called off.

Marcial Mesa discovered the grave and dutifully reported it to the local authorities. Dr. Davis, the same man who had testified at Chacón's trial; W.T. Johnson; Herman Keppler; William Romley; and W.E. Beck returned with Mesa to the site. The body was exhumed and brought to Morenci, and a coroner's inquest was conducted, with Justice of the Peace James Langerman presiding over the investigation. "[F]rom the clothing and other evidence," the body was identified as that of John Miller. The newspaper did not report how Mr. Miller came to his death.

The *Bulletin* reported further, "His disappearance occurred only a few days prior to the killing of Salcido by A. Chacón and his band of robbers and murderers. Foul play was suspected by Miller's friends, as he was by no means a favorite with the tough characters in Morenci, who had been stealing horses, robbing dwellings, etc. He was one of the robbers [*sic*] victims, they having broken into his house and stolen a large number of valuable

Territorial Governor Myron Hawley McCord. *Private collection.*

specimens." The newspaper asserted, prior to the discovery of the grave, "The general belief was that Miller was murdered and his body dragged into an abandoned tunnel or thrown into a shaft."

The *Bulletin* implicated Pilar Luna and Leonitas Morales in the crime, stating, "One of the men killed in the fight with officers at the time Salcido lost his life had Miller's rifle, and this strengthened the theory of Miller's death." The newspaper did not specify whether it was Morales or Luna who was in possession of Miller's Winchester or how the weapon was determined to have previously belonged to the dead man. Not that it would matter. The rifle was enough to connect Chacón to the murder of Mr. Miller, and the tale of Chacón killing a prospector and throwing his corpse down a mine shaft became an integral piece of the legend of the outlaw; it continues to be repeated into the modern era.

As the month of September drew to an end, District Attorney Jones sent a message to Governor Myron Hawley McCord, reassuring him Chacón's capture was imminent. According to the *Holbrook Argus*, Jones intimated that Chacón had taken up residence in the Socorro Mountains in Mexico. Where Jones obtained this information is unknown. In fact, there are no "Socorro Mountains" in Mexico. Could District Attorney Jones have meant the San Mateo Mountains in Socorro County, in the New Mexico Territory? Or perhaps the newspaper was misinformed as to the contents of the message sent by the attorney? Whichever the case, the press of the neighboring territory took umbrage at Mr. Wiley's declaration that a notorious Arizona desperado might be hiding in their picturesque mountains, and a brief bout of editorial fisticuffs followed.

The *Lordsburg Liberal* invoked the wrath of the *Graham Guardian* when, in early October, the former suggested that Chacón had "been seen several times near Morenci" and that "he makes no particular effort to hide himself" during his visits. "It is supposed," wrote the editor, "that if he is recaptured that he will be able to tell a story that will not be very complimentary to the officials of Graham county, and as the officers do not want this story told, they are not very anxious to recapture him." The *Liberal* concluded, saying, "A pull with the officers is a good thing to have, sometimes." Much to the consternation of the Graham County officials, this editorial was reprinted in both the *Arizona Republican* and the *Arizona Silver Belt*.

After quoting the article verbatim, the *Guardian* branded it as "a very grave accusation to bring against an officer or a set of officers," particularly those employed by the Graham County Sheriff's Office, and declared that such recrimination was completely "uncalled for." The editor of the *Guardian*, John J. Birdno, stated most emphatically that Chacón had not been anywhere near Morenci, citing the fact there was a $700 bounty on his head. Editor Birdno then turned the tables on the *Liberal* correspondent and its informant, asking, "If [the officers] are all standing together to prevent his capture, as the *Liberal* intimates, why do not some of the Grant county officials capture him and get the reward? Or, why did not the *Liberal*'s informant capture him?"[23]

Four days after Editor Birdno's statement appeared, the *Tombstone Prospector* reported that "a trio of Mexicans" who had been operating in the area had "added another chapter to their career in crime" when on the previous Sunday afternoon, they assaulted freighter Ben Moore, who was returning to Pearce alone on horseback. "The Mexicans commanded a halt, and enforced the order by presentation of Winchesters." Moore, who had $300 on his person from the sale of his teams, attempted to flee, but a shot from one of the bandits took the horse from beneath him. The horse stumbled and went down, and Moore was pinned beneath the dead animal, with his left leg broken in two places. "In his helpless condition, the robbers searched their victim and secured $210 in money."

The trio had been afoot when they commanded Moore to stop, but after robbing him, the three mounted up and took off in the direction of Clifton, "where they have friends." Moore lay there beneath the horse for several hours before he was discovered. Once he was rescued and told his story, a wire was sent to Cochise County sheriff Scott White in Pearce, who set out immediately to intercept the outlaw trio. In an update to the story, the Tombstone newspaper stated that Moore had been brought into the hospital that town and was interviewed by a representative from the *Prospector*.

The story Moore told the reporter differed from the first reports in some of the details. Moore stated that "the Mexicans" had not actually commanded him to stop, but rather had simply opened fire on him, frightening his horse, which bolted, only "to stumble in a deep road track." Moore broke his leg when he was thrown from the animal. Being incapacitated and looking up into the barrels of the bandits' Winchesters,

Moore readily surrendered his $210 to them. The trio spoke for a moment among themselves and then departed.

There was no mention of Chacón's name in connection with robbery in this first reporting, either by the newspaper or by Mr. Moore. However, by the following day, the trio of "Mexicans" had grown into "a gang of horse thieves," and said gang was now under the auspices of none other than Augustine Chacón. How Chacón's name came to be associated with the robbery of Moore—literally overnight—remains a mystery, but his seemingly random connection to equally random events would become all the more frequent as Chacón's legend continued to grow.

Sheriff White was in disagreement with the *Prospector*'s initial report on the holdup. He did not believe that the three men who robbed Mr. Moore were "the same gang as the Tombstone horse thieves, although the descriptions nearly tally." White had "good reason to believe" that the horse thieves were Francisco Montano and Antonio Luna, a pair of "jail birds who served terms in the county jail and were discharged." The lawman further held that the robbery of Moore was committed by "none other than a gang of desperadoes headed by Chacón, the Graham county murderer." What led Sheriff White to conclude that the culprit had been Chacón was not revealed in the report.

The following day, the *Prospector* reported that officers were still in the field searching for the "Tombstone horse thieves or the Chacón band who held-up Ben Moore." News of this incident was disseminated throughout the territory and was reported in the *Arizona Republican*, the *Graham Guardian*, the *Arizona Daily Star* and the *Holbrook Argus*, all with varying degrees of accuracy. It was the *Daily Star* that revealed that Moore had not recognized Chacón as one of his assailants at the time of the robbery but "now believes it to have been done by Chacón." One must wonder what evidence was presented to him that convinced Moore it was indeed Chacón who had robbed him, as well as how Moore would have known Chacón to be able to state so positively that it was him. Were Moore and Chacón previously acquainted, or was Moore shown a photograph by the local officers after the fact, as were Dolph Wilson and John Stewart of Graham County?

The editor and proprietor of the *Tombstone Prospector*, William Hattich, falsely charged Chacón with an entirely new crime on October 22: armed robbery. The newspaper reported that the evening before, Sheriff White had received notification "that the store belonging to Mrs. [Minta S.] Fervent at San Simeon was held up" and undisclosed amount of cash made off with by the robbers. Deputy Otto Moore was dispatched to investigate the robbery, "and deputy officers in that section placed on look out." Wrote Hattich, without the benefit of any corroborating evidence, "It is not known who the robbers are, but it is not unlikely the work of Chacón and his gang."

This report was carried in *The Tombstone Epitaph*, which Hattich also edited, two days later, and by the *Republican* on the twenty-eighth of the month. Oddly, there was no subsequent news or follow-up stories about the robbery of Mrs. Fervent's store in any of the territorial newspapers. This one item, repeated in the three aforementioned newspapers, is all the information extant.[24]

While on the subject of uncorroborated stories, perhaps this would be an opportune time to address the second story of Chacón and Sheriff John Horton Slaughter.

This particular tale first appeared in *Tombstone's Yesterdays* by Lorenzo D. Walters, published in 1928. In Walters's fantastical book, after escaping from the Graham County calaboose, Chacón befriended another man of Hispanic decent, and they, "being without funds, held up the Solomonville Stage and headed for Old Mexico." En route, Chacón and his partner rode through Cochise County, where they allegedly met up with Sheriff Slaughter. To say that Walters was vague about what occurred between the parties is an understatement: "[W]hen the festivities attending said meeting were over, Chacón once more turned his attention to making tracks with the heel prints pointing northward, but he was all by his lonesome. As the outlaw who was killed wore a heavy beard, it was thought for some time Sheriff Slaughter had killed Chacón, but subsequent events proved that such thoughts were in error as Chacón was positively located across the International Line."

As with the tales penned by Walter Burns and Allen Erwin, the most obvious issue with Walters's story is the timeline. As noted earlier, Slaughter was the Cochise County sheriff from 1886 to 1890, and Chacón did not escape from the Solomonville jail until 1897. Further, there was only one stage robbery in Graham County in 1897, which occurred on July 9 of that year and, for which, the driver, Charles Colbath, and Joseph "Joe" Chrain were indicted by a U.S. grand jury. Colbath and Chrain fled the territory and were never apprehended or tried.

Walters's story was not as preposterous as Burns's and Erwin's tales, but the errors within make it extremely suspect, to the point that it should be considered by the discerning reader to be just another tall tale, with no basis in fact.[25]

While Chacón continued to elude the authorities, his alleged confederates and compatriots were not faring as well. On November 3, the *Arizona Weekly*

Journal-Miner reported that on Friday, October 24, near the smelter in Clifton, an unnamed "Mexican" was found "shot through the neck and his head beaten to a jelly with a rock." Juan Madera was arrested as a suspect in the murder, "given a preliminary examination and bound over to the grand jury." On Sunday morning, a "mob of infuriated Mexicans" entered the jail, dragged Madera outside and riddled him with bullets. Madera was also suspected of killing a second man, whose corpse was east of Clifton, on the road to Duncan. The Prescott newspaper alleged that Madera was a "friend of the murderer Chacón." The *Arizona Daily Citizen*, which had reported the story of the lynching six days earlier, said that Madera was "supposed to be a member of the Chacón gang."[26]

After he was mentioned in connection with the robbery of freighter Ben Moore and the lynching of Juan Madera in Clifton, Augustine Chacón disappears from the historical record for almost a year. In large part, this lack of media coverage may have been due to the escalation of U.S. tensions with Spain over the continuing Spanish occupation of the island of Cuba. These tensions would culminate in the Spanish-American War, which lasted about four months, from April 21 to August 13, 1898. Prior to the war being declared, the territorial newspapers, like most the newspapers across the country, were filled with jingoistic rhetoric and propaganda. Additionally, the territorial newspapers were featuring numerous stories about Colonel Theodore Roosevelt's First Volunteer Cavalry, also known as the "Rough Riders," and its many members who came out of the Arizona Territory.

Colonel Theodore Roosevelt's First Volunteer Cavalry, aka the "Rough Riders." *Library of Congress.*

Less than a month after Spain conceded defeat and sued for peace, Augustine Chacón made a brief reappearance in the newspapers. On September 1, the *Los Angeles Times* reported that one Charles Johnson rode into Clifton on August 20 to file a complaint with Deputy Sheriff Benjamin R. "Ben" Clark. Johnson claimed that Chacón and two confederates had stolen "a lot of horses" from his ranch.

In response to the complaint, Deputy Clark formed a posse and rode with Johnson back out to his ranch. From the ranch, the posse followed the trail of the horse thieves into the Black Mountains. "The chase was short-lived, however, as Clark, while following the trail on the top of Black Mountains, was badly injured in the back and shoulders, his horse falling with him." The deputy sheriff was taken to the C.A. Bar ranch, where he caught a train back to Clifton. "He has been confined to his bed ever since."

After more succinctly reporting the same information, the editor of the *Lordsburg Liberal* quipped, "Taking into consideration the way Chacón escaped, it would not be showing proper courtesy to a brother officer for any Graham county deputy sheriff to arrest him again, even for horse stealing." Tersely, the *Holbrook Argus* stated, "Chacón, the murderer who escaped jail at Clifton last year, and two confederates stole a number of horses near that town, and were trailed into the Black mountains by officers." Oddly, the Graham County papers made no mention of the incident.

However, the *Los Angeles Times* took great interest in what was going on in and around Graham County, as on September 20, the newspapers reported that a "band of woodchoppers working in the vicinity of Ash Springs" had managed to draw the attention of someone with their "suspicious actions." This someone—who remained anonymous—went to the law, and "a strong sheriff's posse" was dispatched to investigate. The posse, reported the *Times*, "was happily disappointed in not running across the outlaw, Augustin Chacón, as anticipated."[27]

And then Chacón disappeared from the historical record once more, this time for a period of about six months. At least, he disappeared from the pages of the territorial newspapers. It should be recalled, especially in reading the various contemporary accounts in this chapter and the next, that on the gallows, Chacón offered a plausible alibi for his whereabouts during this period. He stated that immediately after his escape, he "went to the Yaqui river and enlisted as a soldier at the time the soldiers were there. I was there as a soldier." Chacón also stated that he was "honorably discharged from the Mexican army, which would seem to imply he served out a full term of enlistment.

Regarding his alleged sojourns into the United States at the head of a band of desperadoes and the various crimes the newspapers charged him with committing, he flatly denied them, declaring, "I have been told by several people that I have been in this country since I got away from here. I was here four years ago, myself with another party.…I was here for the purpose of knowing how my business was getting on and to hear what was being said about me. That is why I came here—I did not come here to do any wrong or harm anybody." Chacón continued in his disavowal, saying, "I have been told that I have been here since, at different places at different times, with a band of twenty men, and that I have been seen here and there with a band of twenty men. This is not so. At the time I heard this report, I was a long distance from here."[28]

CHAPTER 5

THE LEGEND EVOLVES

The next time Augustine Chacón's name appeared in the territorial newspapers was in March 1899; it was not in connection with some crime that had been committed, but rather in the context of a political debate. Benjamin Clark, the former deputy and new Graham County sheriff, petitioned Governor Nathan Oakes Murphy to offer monetary rewards for the recapture of escaped prisoners out of the territorial budget. The editor of the *Arizona Weekly Journal-Miner*, John C. Martin, thought such a suggestion was absurd: "We have heard before of a sheriff charging a county for recapturing prisoners who got away from him. The fee system for sheriffs works like a charm."

When Governor Murphy refused the request, the *Graham Guardian* and the *Solomonville Bulletin* accused him "of all kinds of deep designs." Editor John Birdno of the *Guardian* assumed that the new governor, a Republican, "desires to hit Graham county an upper cut, presumably to show the people of the Gila valley that he doesn't think much of a county that will pile up a democratic majority such as comes from Graham every two years." The *Bulletin* believed that the refusal was the result of an animosity between the governor and Councilman Olney because the latter voted "against measures Governor Murphy champions."

These responses led to a prolonged editorial argument between the Graham County newspapers and others throughout the territory, including the *Safford Arizonian*, the *Arizona Republican* and the *Arizona Gazette*. The editor of the *Arizonian* asserted, "If our contemporaries will look in to the matter a little, they will find it is not customary for the territory to offer a reward for criminals who escape from county jails until every effort possible has been made by county officials to recapture them." Editor Birdno replied, "If our brother editor will look over his files, he will find therein a reward offered for the capture of Chacón. This reward was offered by Gov. McCord as soon as the request was made."

In fact, notices of a reward of $500 for the apprehension of Chacón had appeared in the *Florence Tribune* and the *Graham Guardian* from June 1897 until January 1898. These notices specifically addressed Chacón's escape from the jail at Solomonville and were authorized by Governor Franklin. Just as Birdno had argued, there was a precedent for the territorial government offering of a reward for apprehension of a criminal who had escaped custody from a county calaboose.

Alas, Governor Murphy must have changed his mind, at least in regards to a certain escapee, as on March 29, the *Arizona Daily Star*, the *Tombstone Prospector* and the *Weekly Orb* (Bisbee) reported that a proclamation had been issued authorizing the payment of a reward of $300 "for the arrest of Augustin Chacón." The *Daily Star* added, "Chacón is a tough citizen, and his return to durance will be a social blessing."[29]

If the territorial officials and officers expected that an offer of a $300 reward would result in the apprehension of Augustine Chacón, they were sadly mistaken. The notices failed to generate renewed interest in the case at all. Chacón was conspicuously absent for the territorial newspapers until mid-November, when the *Willcox News* ran the following item:

> *Augustin Chacón, the leader of the band of thieves and smugglers on the border, has defied posses now in quest of him to effect his capture. It will be remembered that this is the same man who while under sentence of death in Graham county escaped from the jail.*

It was a relatively short notice, but it effectively renewed the interest of the territorial press in Chacón's case. This notice would be reprinted verbatim in the *Arizona Republican* on November 19, in the *Arizona Silver Belt* and the *Winslow Mail* on November 23, in the *Arizona Daily Orb* on December 2, in the *Tombstone Prospector* on December 5, in *The Tombstone Epitaph* on December 10, again in the *Republican* on December 12 and in the *Copper Era* and again in the *Silver Belt* on December 14.

It could be argued that the legend of Chacón—which, up to this juncture, was based primarily on his conviction for the murder of Pablo Salcido and his subsequent escape from the Solomonville jail—began to take on a life of its own, without regard for what Chacón was actually doing. From this point forward, no matter how fantastic and implausible the tale the press came up with, it was reported as absolute fact and was reprinted again and again.[30]

The Blue Nose Canyon Fight

The *Los Angeles Times* began this process of legend-building in late November, reporting the Chacón and his gang had been "lately surprised by Nogales officers near Harshaw," resulting in the deaths of two of his men. The outlaw then sent word to the posse, specifically Captain Hathaway and Deputy Sheriff Flewelling, that he would "get them" if they came within a distance of one thousand yards of him. Captain Hathaway, reported the *Times*, was undaunted by Chacón's threats and vowed to continue to hunt the bandit in the "usual haunts." Chacón, it was said, was wanted more by the Mexican authorities than he was by authorities "on the northern side of the line, and it is probable he will remain a resident of Santa Cruz county until finally bagged by the officers of the law."

A check of contemporary newspapers in Arizona for the last three months of 1899 did turn up a story in the *Border Vidette* about Captain J.L. Hathaway, a U.S. customs inspector, and William W. Flewelling, a Santa Cruz County deputy sheriff, being involved in a firefight with "a band of desperadoes and smugglers" that left two of the latter party dead. These outlaws had been "terrorizing the settlers in the valleys and mining camps in the Patagonia mountains" and had become "unbearable to the settlers," who turned to the federal officers for help. Inspector Hathaway assembled a posse of five well-armed men, including Deputy Flewelling.

In the early morning hours of Tuesday, October 17, the posse surprised the bandits in their camp in Blue Nose Canyon, two and a half miles from Harshaw. The suspects had already awoken and appeared to be preparing to cook breakfast, with some standing about the campfire and one mixing flour for tortillas. When officers commanded the suspects to throw up their hands, the men broke and ran for cover, except for the one who had been mixing the flour, who "coolly began to remove the dough that adhered to his hands." The newspaper reported that the first shot was fired by one of the suspects, which was answered by a shot from Deputy Flewelling's revolver. Then the firefight became general and lasted about ten minutes.

Captain James L. "Jim" Hathaway, U.S. Customs. *Arizona Historical Society, PC 1000, Main Photo Collection, Portraits—Hathaway, James L. (Jim), #76050.*

When the smoke cleared in Blue Nose Canyon, one of the suspected bandits, Cruz Marquez, lay dead, shot through the head. Another suspect, later identified as Domingo Vidal—the man of the doughy hands—had been mortally wounded but had still managed to escape with his companions. The officers, none of whom were wounded in the melee, then set about collecting evidence at the campsite. Captain Hathaway reportedly found the severed heads "of upwards of 100 cattle that had been butchered by the outlaws," in addition to "a rifle…a horse, two burros, four pack saddles, two Mexican riding saddles, and two sacks of provisions."

As far as can be determined, this report in the *Border Vidette* was the only in-depth coverage of the incident at Blue Nose Canyon by a territorial newspaper. The article ran nearly two full columns and, it may be safely assumed, was garnered from eyewitness accounts told to the *Vidette* reporter by one or more of the officers involved. Nowhere in this lengthy and exceedingly detailed report was Augustine Chacón's name mentioned. How, then, did the *Los Angeles Times* come to connect Chacón to this gang of smugglers and rustlers?[31]

The Morenci Laundry-House Murders

When three Chinese immigrants were murdered on the evening of April 18, 1900, in the laundry they ran in the town of Morenci, the *Graham Guardian* reported the following day, "No clue had yet been obtained as to who the murderers were." When the *El Paso Times* reported on this triple murder in Morenci on April 22, it supposed the motive for the killing to have been robbery, but stated that no arrests had yet been made. Two day later, the *El Paso Herald* reported that there were still no clues as to the identity of the killer(s), and details relating to the murders were few. The *Copper Era & Morenci Leader* published its account of the murders on April 26, stating everything in the laundry of any value that had been stolen and that the victims had been robbed of about $300 in cash. The newspaper also included portions of the official coroner's inquest report, filed by Justice of the Peace Antony Wright of Precinct 3.

On April 19, Justice Wright received a telephone call instructing him to travel to Morenci to hold an inquest. Upon arriving in town, he was informed that three Chinese residents—Louis Fat, Ar Ohock and Hong Yick—had been slain the evening before, and he was escorted to the scene of the crime. Once inside the laundry, Justice Wright was confronted with a most gruesome sight. All three of the victims had been "shot in the head, two apparently having been killed while still in bed. The house had been thoroughly ransacked for valuables, showing that robbery was probably the motive of the crime."

Upon further examination, it was discovered that at least eight shots had been fired during the robbery. "[A]lthough the house was situated in the midst of a thickly settled neighborhood, only one person could be found who had heard any shots fired." This person was Adelia Hernandez, who stated that she had heard gunfire and had told one of the other women in the neighborhood about it. Juan Anchonda also testified at the inquest, saying that he was coming home from work when he saw two suspicious-looking men leaving the scene of the murder and heading off in the direction of the Lone Star Mine. Anchonda could not positively identify the men.

After the coroner's inquest was completed and the bodies of Fat, Ohock and Yick were prepared for burial, they were interred at the South Clifton Cemetery "by their brethren in Morenci and Clifton, in the usual style peculiar to the religious customs of the Chinese people." The newspaper did report that a suspect had been arrested in the case but did not elaborate further. There was no mention of Augustine Chacón either by the county newspapers or in Justice Wright's report.

When the *Evening Times* (Washington D.C.), the *St. Louis Globe Democrat*, the *Naugatuck (CT) Daily News* and the *Marion (OH) Star* published their accounts on April 25, the columns were suffused with grisly details about the murders and unsubstantiated accusations about the identity of the killers. Under the blatantly racist headline "Three Chinks," the reporter for the *Marion Star* revealed that two of the men had been shot in the head while still in bed, "while the third had made a desperate fight for his life." The Ohio newspaper stated that the premises had been ransacked and "several thousand in coin" taken. The *Naugatuck Daily News* reported virtually the same story but added that the man who had fought back had been "shot several times, the fatal bullet being fired at such close range as almost to tear off the side of his head." Except for the headlines, the reports provided in the *Evening Times* and the *St. Louis Globe-Democrat* were exactly the same.

The *Evening Times*, the *Daily News* and the *Globe-Democrat* asserted, "A dozen Mexican families living in the immediate vicinity affirmed they heard nothing during the night, but have plainly been terrorized. There is no doubt the murders were done by the Chacón band of Mexican assassins, several of its members having been lately seen in this vicinity." The *Marion Star* also accused "the Chacón band of Mexican assassins" of committing the crime.

The next day, the *Owensboro Messenger-Inquirer* of Kentucky published the Associated Press version of the story—the same that had been published in the *Evening Times*, the *Daily News* and the *Globe-Democrat* the day before. The "Chacón gang" was again implicated in the crime. However, the most sensational of the reports connecting Chacón to the murders came two days later, from the *Los Angeles Times.* This newspaper took what had been a paragraph-long item in these other newspapers and turned it into half a column of remarkably xenophobic hyperbole.

In keeping with the contemporary racist beliefs about the inherent degeneracy of the Chinese people, the *Times* said of the victims, "like all Chinese they gambled." The newspaper alleged that the night before the murder, the three men had visited "Slagtown," where they had won "considerable money" at the gambling tables. "This probably furnished the motive for the crime, as two trunks were broken open and the laundry thoroughly ransacked." The *Times* also alluded to the victims' use of opium, saying that one of the men had died with a pipe in his hand.

Further, adhering to the tenets of lurid sensationalism and crude exaggeration that were hallmarks of this newspaper during this period, the *Los Angeles Times* article did not hesitate in disclosing the grisliest of details relating to the murders, stating that the two men who were found in bed were shot at such close quarters that their faces were "powder burned." Further, the one who had put up a struggle against his assailants was reportedly shot through the left eye, the bullet "tearing off the entire side of his head." The three men were said to have been discovered the following day, "weltering in their own blood," and there were "splattered blood and brains scattered about the room."

Although the *Times* readily admitted, "No clew [*sic*] is known, and the coroner's jury says 'died from pistol shots from hands of people unknown,'" the author of the article did not refrain from asserting, "The many mysterious murders in the vicinity, and the fact that members of the gang have been seen in Clifton, lead many to believe that the notorious Chacón band of outlaws is again in the vicinity."

Again, the question arises as to how and why the *Los Angeles Times*, and the other newspapers previously mentioned, had come to connect Chacón's name to these brutal murders?

As evidenced by the published reports about the Blue Nose Canyon Incident and the Morenci Laundry-House Murders, one can see that Chacón's name was beginning to become attached to any crime committed (or was even suspected to have been committed) by a person or persons of Hispanic heritage, without corroborating evidence of any kind. None of the officers involved in the Blue Nose Canyon shootout, nor Justice Wright, who investigated the Laundry-House Murders, even alluded to Chacón's involvement in these events. Yet the national press did not hesitate in implicating Chacón.

It may be tempting to put these insinuations down to "yellow journalism," which was ubiquitous in the newspapers of the late nineteenth century. The elements of this style of journalism are present and easily identified in the aforementioned articles, including the use of scare headlines, the sensationalizing of the stories, morbidly graphic descriptions, unverified statements, undisclosed sources and the unsubstituted accusations of complicity or guilt. However, this still does not explain how Chacón came to be singled out by the national newspapers as the prime mover behind these criminal enterprises.

For the answer to this question, one need only look to the Arizona territorial newspapers and the publication in November 1899 of the report alleging that Chacón was "the leader of the band of thieves and smugglers on the border." By advancing this villainous caricature of the man, the territorial press had, in essence, served the rest of the nation up a brand-new heavyweight desperado, evocative of legendary outlaws like Jesse James, Joaquin Murrieta and Billy the Kid, replete with a resonant and catchy moniker: Chacón!

Better yet, at least from the press's perspective, Chacón was Hispanic—a Mexican—and this allowed the media to capitalize (literally) on the prejudices and bigotry of the preponderant Anglo culture. In time, Chacón would come to embody the very essence of Anglo America's anxieties about Hispanics, as well as the odious traits that were regularly attributed to them by racist Anglos: their inherent degeneracy, their lack of honor and morality, their laziness and indolence, their ignorance, their cruelty, their superstitions and pagan beliefs and their proclivities toward violence, sensuality and debauchery.

It is no wonder, during this age of "yellow journalism," that the national media was so quick to seize on the territorial newspapers' contrived depiction of Augustine Chacón as an up-and-coming bandit chieftain and further expound on it. Chacón made for good copy. With the dawn of the new century, it seemed as if the halcyon days of the mounted outlaw gangs—the James-Younger Gang, the High Fives Gang, the Doolin-Dalton Gang, the Cochise County Cowboys, the Sam Bass Gang and others—had passed into history, but the wild and woolly Arizona Territory (specifically the press) had been thoughtful enough to provide one more criminal horde, and a Hispanic one at that. What could be better? The only surprise is how long it took the territorial newspapers to avail themselves of this mythic Mexican monster that they had sired.[32]

The New River Station Murders

Less than a month after the Morenci Laundry-House Murders, Chacón was reported by the *Arizona Silver-Belt* to be "making his home in the vastness of the mountains along Eagle creek, and is supplied with provisions, ammunition, etc. by his friends in Morenci." Then, on Thursday evening, June 7, 1900, thirty-five-year-old Anton Olsen and his partner, Charles Stewart, the proprietors of the New River Station, located twenty miles to the north of Phoenix on the Cattle Creek road, were found to have been murdered. John Hughes discovered the bodies. "Olsen had been shot twice, once in the left breast and once in the neck. Stewart had been shot in the left breast." The motive for the murders was thought to have been robbery, as "the station was pillaged." The *Arizona Republican* was the first to break the story, intelligence concerning the crime having been brought into the Maricopa County Sheriff's Office on Friday, June 8, by Ray Tompkinson of Frog Tanks.

Tompkinson alleged that the crime had been perpetrated by "four Mexicans," the same who had tried to assassinate a prospector named W.H. Rice the night before the double homicide occurred. Tompkinson said that the news had been brought to Frog Tanks, a distance of about nine miles, by Mr. Rice and Yavapai County deputy sheriff Daniel Nelson, who had been out searching for Rice's assailants. When interviewed later, Rice stated that Tompkinson was mistaken, saying that the news had been brought to Frog Tanks by Hughes, who had been camped on the property, and was likely there the afternoon the murders occurred. Mr. Rice believed that Hughes knew about the murders but "must have been afraid to tell."

After learning about crime, Mr. Rice and Deputy Nelson proceeded directly from Frog Tanks to the New River Station, where they found a "pitiful sight." Olsen was dead, lying out in the yard in front of the station. Stewart's body was found in the backyard. Each had a dog lying beside him, which "greeted the strangers with joyous barks." Rice and Deputy Nelson did not disturb the crime scene but immediately "set out on the trail of the Mexicans," even though the tracks were nearly twenty-four hours old. The trail led to the Arizona Canal at Sunset, near the Moody Saloon, just north of Phoenix. "A woman saw [the suspects] there, and said a Mexican in front of the saloon asked them to have a drink, but they refused." Rice and Nelson lost the trail of the quartet near the intersection of the Castle Creek and Black Canyon roads.

A salesman named Van Kirk, who was in the habit of visiting the New River Station twice weekly, declared that he had seen the suspects on the road on the day of the killings. It was stated that their general countenance was "so villainous that Van Kirk's attention was attracted," and he said he had "warned Olsen and Stewart to be on their guard." Van Kirk described one of the suspects "as a thick, heavy set man, with a long heavy moustache, and a growth of stubby whiskers." This "meager description" was included in the "telephone and telegraph messages [that] had been sent out in every direction."

Gila County sheriff William T. Armstrong happened to be in Phoenix when word of the murders was received at the Maricopa County Sheriff's Office, having returned from the town of Weaver. Sheriff Armstrong reported that there had recently been a burglary at Pasqual (Nigro's) place in Globe, which was said to have been committed by "four strange Mexicans, one of whom closely answers the description of the man who attracted the attention of Van Kirk."

The *Republican* reported that "a party, consisting of George McFall, William Wilson, and Tompkinson" was accompanying "Merryman & Halley's dead wagon" back out to the New River Station to retrieve the bodies of Anton Olsen and Charles Stewart and return them to Phoenix for examination by County Coroner C.W. Johnstone. Meanwhile, Maricopa County sheriff David L. Murray, Deputy Sheriff Charles Slankard, Deputy Sheriff Nelson of Yavapai and Mr. Rice formed a posse to go out in search of the perpetrators once more, in the hope of discovering new clues that might aid in locating and capturing them.

In its follow-up report, published on June 10, the *Republican* said that before the retrieval team reached the New River Station the night before, they had been assailed "by a horrible stench." The bodies of the two victims, having been left where they lay by Mr. Rice and Deputy Nelson, had begun to decompose under the sweltering Arizona sun. "They were horribly swollen and disfigured," reported the newspaper, "for the chickens had gathered about them, and the vultures, and the unclean beasts of the desert." The members of the expedition stated that "it was an errand which they could not be induced to undertake again." The newspaper gave no indication of what had become of the faithful dogs that had been watching over the bodies of their masters.

John Hughes received the censure of the newspaper, which stated, "[E]ither through selfishness or fear, [he] had neglected to give information of the death of these men, whereby the authorities would have been given an

Pinal County sheriff William C. Truman. *Pinal County Historical Society #5178.*

advantage of not less than twelve hours in the pursuit of the murderers." As it was, when Sheriff Murray next contacted his office, he had nothing new to report regarding the pursuit and "inquired if information had reached the office from any other source." Although there had been messages, none was deemed particularly helpful to the investigation.

Pinal County sheriff William C. Truman had telephoned the Maricopa Sheriff's Office saying he had no doubt that "the gang of four Mexican outlaws" who had camped for a month alongside Mineral Creek in his jurisdiction matched the description of the murderers he had been given. He, too, believed they were the same men who robbed Pasqual's store in Globe. The *Republican* further elaborated on the description of the robbers, revealing that "two rode bay horses, one a sorrel, and one a buckskin." The four men were reported to be well-armed with revolvers and Winchesters, and one was wearing a sombrero.

The *Republican* stopped short of naming Chacón as one of the suspects, but the paper certainly made a blatant allusion to his involvement, saying, "The murderers are believed to be members of a gang of nine desperate

Chihuahua Mexicans, who operated about Clifton for several years. Five were killed in one way or another, and the leader was captured, tried at Solomonville, convicted, and sentenced to be hanged. On the night before his execution, he broke jail." The newspaper went on to accuse "the leader" of "twenty killings in this territory and Sonora," including among his alleged victims three women. "It is supposed he is the short, stout man with the long moustache and stubby black beard described by Van Kirk and the others."

Of course, at five feet, eight inches, Chacón was about average height, and as evidenced by existing photographs and previously published descriptions, he was not overweight. But these facts hardly mattered.

To the credit of its editor, John C. Martin, when the *Arizona Journal-Miner* reported on the murders in its June 13 edition, there was no mention of or allusions to Chacón's involvement. In fact, the newspaper avoided altogether the use of the word *gang*, saying only that "the murderers are supposed to be Mexican." On page eight of the same issue, the *Journal-Miner* provided an update on the progress of the manhunt, saying that there were "three determined posses" out on the suspects' trail. "The murderers are now on the Pinal range, a vast desert stretch of country, surrounded on all sides by settlements…[t]hey are headed a little north of east, which will run them right into the worst place they could choose for escaping, as the settlements are thickest there, and everyone is on the watch for them."

Governor Murphy, in his "Proclamation of Reward" announcement (first published in the *Arizona Republican* on June 13), and Maricopa County sheriff Murphy, in his reward announcement (published in the same edition of the newspaper on the same day), both avoided any speculation about the identity or even the ethnicity of the killers. The territory offered a bounty of $500 for the killer(s) of Olsen and Stewart, while the Maricopa County Board of Supervisors was more generous, offering $200 per head "for the arrest and conviction of the murderers."

In contrast to the *Republican*, which only alluded to Chacón's involvement in the New River Station murders, the *Florence Tribune* blatantly accused the man. "There is little doubt now that the 'short, heavy set man of the four' is Chacón, the murderer of twenty men and women, the leader of the slaughtering band." Van Kirk had been shown a photograph of Chacón (presumably the one taken after his arrest in Morenci), and when directly asked "if he had ever seen anybody that liked like the photograph," Van Kirk stated that he had seen the man the previous Thursday on the road to the New River Station.

Portrait of Augustine Chacón that appeared in the *Arizona Republican*. *Author's collection.*

Despite the dearth of evidence to support the assertions about Chacón's involvement in the New River Station homicides, the *Arizona Republican* did not retract its previous statements. Instead, in its June 18 edition, the newspaper doubled down on its insinuations of June 9, putting Augustine Chacón on the first page and featuring a crudely drawn portrait of the man. The caption below this rudimentary rendering was equally appalling in its revilement and defamation of its subject:

> *Augustin Chacón, believed to be the leader of the band of four Mexicans who killed Olsen and Stewart at New River Wells, is said to have a mania for murder and a record of twenty victims. He is a native of Chihuahua and a price was set on his head by the government of Mexico. He had committed several murders in Chihuahua and Sonora, three of his victims being women. He arrived in Morenci about five years ago and is believed to have committed many murders in that neighborhood. He was convicted of one at Solomonville, and sentenced to be hanged. On the night before the day fixed for his execution, he escaped from jail in a more or less mysterious manner. He was known for some time after to be at the head of a band of outlaws in the mountains of eastern Graham county. The band which Chacón drew around him after his escape consisted of eight men, of whom five have been killed. The other three and the leader are believed to be the men who committed the New River crime, who had six months before burglarized a store in Globe, and then went into rendezvous on Mineral creek in Pinal county.*

One may wonder at the recurring use of the word *believed* in the foregoing caption ("Augustin Chacón, *believed* to be the leader of the band of four Mexicans," "He…is *believed* to have committed many murders in that neighborhood," "The other three and the leader are *believed* to be the men who committed the New River crime") and think that this might well have been a stratagem on the part of the author to allow him to make outlandish accusations without actually having to take responsibility for the fact that none of them was true. But who would the author have to answer to for disseminating disinformation? It was not as though Chacón would be suing him for libel.

More likely it was a machination designed to sway public opinion. The author never stated who "believed" these statements to be true—only that they were "believed." The "who" was implied. It could be many persons or just one. The reader was purposely left uninformed. However, by the utilization of this term, the inference was made that the person or persons who believed these statements to be true were better informed about the subject than the reader was. It also implied a certain authority on the subject—that this was the belief of law enforcement officers, public officials, investigators, journalists and/or the general public—and that the unenlightened reader should trust that these statements were concordant with facts and evidence and should also believe them.

The use of the term *believed* was a calculated manipulation on the part the author designed to influence the opinion of the reader and to bring the reader into agreement with the author's assertions. Unlike the newspapers of today, which must compete with television, radio and the internet to disseminate their message, the newspapers of the late nineteenth century absolutely dominated the media and supplied the majority of news and information consumed by the public. They became quite adept in the shaping of public opinion and controlling public discourse. This overarching influence of the newspapers may clearly be seen in the continuing case of Augustine Chacón.

There was a second article in the aforementioned edition of the *Republican* concerning the murders, though relegated to the fifth page. It spoke to the continuing manhunt for the suspects in the New River Station murders. The posse out of Phoenix—consisting of Deputy Slankard, Deputy Nelson, W.H. Rice, Charlie Mullen and John Woolf—had struck the trail of the suspects near the mining community of Goldfield, to the east of Phoenix, at the base of the Superstition Mountain Range, and followed it more than fifty miles to the town of Globe. There, on the afternoon of June 13, they met the posse headed by Sheriff Murray.

The following morning, the posses merged, and "Deputies Slankard and [William "Billy"] Moore of Phoenix, Deputy Vores of Globe, Pete Spence, Constable George McGee, and John Woolf continued on in the pursuit, in the direction of Pinal Creek, which was the last reported place the suspects had camped." The remainder of the two posses, including Sheriff Murray, made their way back home. The *Republican* reported, "The outlaws are now in a country where they will be pretty apt to keep the officers guessing, unless they can strike a hot trail and keep it warm." The newspaper revealed that despite the fact Sheriff Murray had "ascertained some facts in connection with the affair," the identities of the three other men were still a mystery. Still, the lawman maintained Chacón was the leader of the gang, stating that he had been "pretty well identified, through his picture, by Van Kirk."

After the publication of the preceding reports, the territorial newspapers lost interest in the case. The reward announcements continued to be printed in the *Arizona Republican* and the *Graham Guardian*, but there were few news items concerning the investigation. The *San Francisco Chronicle* reported on June 20 that three of "the Mexican bandits who committed the double murder at New River Springs" had been killed in a "bloody battle" near the Black Warrior Mine, and the fourth member of the gang and been captured. "A dispatch from Globe says Charlie Slankard, Bill Moore, Pete Spence, and other notable trailers came in to Globe today [June 18] with a vicious looking Mexican, heavily ironed."

The territorial papers recorded no such "bloody battle." However, the *Tucson Citizen* reported on the twenty-first that after having been afield a week, Deputy Moore had returned to Phoenix. The deputy revealed that the posse had succeeded in apprehending "a tough character," who was held for two days, but upon providing alibi, he was turned loose. The actual killers were still on the dodge. However, the Maricopa Sheriff's Office assured the public that Deputy Slankard and the posse "were still hot on the trail."

In its June 24 edition, *The Tombstone Weekly Epitaph* reprinted the article previously published by the *Republican* verbatim but omitted the crude rendering of Chacón. The *Graham Guardian* made mention of the "cartoon of Chacón," noting that the rendering was derived "from a photograph taken in the jail yard at Solomonville after he had been sentenced to death." Neither of the newspapers made any mention of Deputy Slankard's posse, and there would be no further news in the territorial press concerning the New River Station murderers, except the continued accusation that Chacón was somehow responsible.

While the Arizona officers continued in their search for the murderers of Olsen and Stewart, the suspected murderers of Chinese immigrants Louis Fat, Ar Ohock and Hong Yick were being apprehended in Texas and returned to Graham County in the custody of Deputy Sheriff James Nicks. The *Western Liberal* reported the capture of the Pedro Herrera and Gaspar Garcia in their edition of June 22. "Mr. Nicks says the evidence against the men is circumstantial, but he is confident he has the right men, and that evidence can be produced that will be enough to hang them." Deputy Nicks further asserted that there was enough evidence "to break up the hard gang that has been making Morenci its headquarters for a longtime." The Lordsburg newspaper stated that the gang in question was "really the remnant of the gang led by Chacón."

Herrera and Garcia, as well as Pedro Subio, who was captured by William E. "Cyclone Bill" Beck near Solomonville, had their preliminary examination before Justice of the Peace W.H. Settle the following week. The *Copper Era* disclosed District Attorney Wiley Jones had no hard evidence against them, "but a chain of circumstantial evidence is would around the prisoners so strongly that there can no doubt of their guilt." However, it was said that part of "the band of cutthroats and thieves" who were "infesting" Morenci had attempted to intimidate the witnesses in the case. "The principle witness, a woman, testifid [*sic*] that her life had been threatened, and pointed out [Enriques] Bustillos as the man who made the threat." Bustillos, described as a "hard and tough character," was subsequently arrested by Sheriff Clark for obstruction of justice.

Herrera, Garcia and Subio were summarily indicted and ordered to be held over until the next term of the court in October. Whether it was due to the witnesses being threatened and therefore refusing to testify on behalf of the prosecution or just a lack of "direct evidence," the case against Herrera, Subio and Garcia was dismissed by the court, and the defendants were allowed to go free. To this day, the case of the Morenci Laundry-House Murders remains unsolved.

On June 28, in one of the few retractions printed by a territorial newspaper concerning allegations made against Chacón, the *Copper Era*, speaking of the New River Wells murders, said, "It was reported that Chacón, who had escaped jail at Solomonville in '97, while under a sentence to hang, is the leader of the gang [that committed the murders], but Sheriff Clark of this county says he is satisfied that this is a mistake." However, the lawman did not entirely exonerate the man, saying that "two of Chacón's Morenci pals are in the gang," implying that Chacón was still thought to be affiliated in some way with the murderers.[33]

The Eagle Creek Murders

William F. Wheeler and his friend, W.H. Howe, both employees of the Detroit Copper Mining Company in Morenci, had left their homes and families in early July to go on a hunting trip in the vicinity of Eagle Creek, with the intention of being out "two or three days." When, after eight to ten days had passed, Mr. Howe's wife "became fearful of their safety and notified Deputy Sheriff Nicks," Deputy Sheriff James R. "Jim" Nicks took to the saddle and went out in search of the two missing men but was unable to locate them. Frustrated, the officer rode back to Morenci, formed a small posse and returned again to Eagle Creek.

Along the way, the posse met up with "some Mexican wood choppers," who said they had seen Wheeler and Howell near the Eagle Creek pumping station and that, from there, the men had headed up along the river. Working from this information, Deputy Nicks and his posse headed up along the river as well but were still unable to find any trace of the two men. "After a prolonged hunt, the party was forced to return home for rest and supplies." By this point, said the correspondent for the *Graham Guardian*, the erstwhile deputy was convinced that the men "had met with foul play."

On Tuesday, July 17, Deputy Nicks resumed his search for Wheeler and Howe. About nine miles from the Eagle Creek pump, the officer observed a large kettle of vultures in the sky and went to investigate. Directly beneath the circling birds, Deputy Nicks found the corpses of the missing men. The bodies were covered in brush, and both had been shot through the head. "The crime is supposed to have been committed by a band of Mexican outlaws who are known to be camped near the place," reported the newspaper, "and are said to be the band who committed the murders at River Wells recently."

On the morning of the twenty-third, Sheriff Clark, accompanied by his deputies, left Solomonville for Morenci with the intent of hunting down the killers of Howe and Wheeler. "Every suspicious character will be taken in and made to give an account of himself," reported the *Arizona Daily Citizen*. Unfortunately, the lawmen had very few clues to work with, but the sheriff had offered a reward of $500 for information leading to the arrest and conviction of the perpetrator(s) and hoped that this "would induce some one to put them on the track of the murderers."

The *Arizona Daily Citizen* would be the first to link Chacón's name to the murders of Wheeler and Howe, saying, "That part of the country is infested with desperate characters, among whom Chacón, the outlaw, is the most notorious." The Tucson-based newspaper would not be the last to impute this.

An unnamed "gentleman" from Solomonville, who had only recently arrived in Phoenix, when interviewed by a correspondent from the *Republican* stated that Sheriff Clark was taking "stringent measures" to bring to heel the outlaw gangs in the area. There were thought to be two separate gangs that had been operating out throughout Gila and Graham counties "for several years." The first of these was "a band of murderous Mexicans" headquartered "in an almost inaccessible section of Eagle Creek." The second was "a band of equally desperate American outlaws" that had been camping along the Black River. "Until those nests of crime are broken up," asserted the *Republican*, "there can be no hope of steady good order."

The murders of Howe and Wheeler—like the murders of Louis Fat, Ar Ohock and Hong Yick and the murders of Anton Olsen and Charles Stewart—would remain unsolved. However, without any corroborating proof or evidence past the accusation made by the reporter from the *Daily Citizen*, the murders of the two men on Eagle Creek have continued to be attributed to Augustine Chacón well into the modern era. The story, presented as absolute fact, can be found repeated (with slight variations) in *Pearson's Magazine* (1905), *Arizona* by McClintock (1916), *Frontier Days in the Southwest* by Ringgold (1952), "The Hairy One" by Rickard (1970), *Outlaw Tales of Arizona* by Jan Cleere (2006), *Arizona Gunfighters* by Yadon & Anderson (2010) and *Outlaw Tales of the Old West* (2016), among others.[34]

One would think that if Chacón were indeed headquartered in the Morenci area, and knew how wanted he was by the authorities (certainly he would have been apprised of the attention being afforded him in the territorial newspapers), he would endeavor to keep a low profile. Despite this, during the week of July 23, an unnamed contractor on the Morenci Southern Railroad made the claim that Chacón himself had ventured into his camp "and got supplies from some of his men." Was it true? Probably not. The first question one might ask would be was the contractor acquainted with Chacón enough to know him by sight? If not, how did he know it was Chacón and not someone else entirely?

Beginning in late June 1900, a singularly imaginative article about Chacón (derived in part from the June 18 story featured in the *Arizona Republican*) began circulating through the Associate Press–affiliated newspapers across the country and continued to be reported time and again for almost a month (with some slight variations), at which time this story was replaced by another even more incredible tale. The former article seems to have first appeared in the *Missoulian* newspaper of Montana. It is reprinted here in its entirety:

> *An Arizona Bandit*
> *Has Killed Twenty-Three People During His Career*
>
> *Tucson special: Juan Chacón, commonly known as "Pelelo," which, according to Mexican palaver, means too insignificant to talk about, and his sanguinary gang of three Mexicans, who killed T.W. Stewart and Anton Olsen at New River Wells a weeks ago, are still at large, and various posses are diligently scouring the country for them, with daily a smaller chance*

of finding them. The gang was trailed from the scene of the murder to the Arizona canal, just north of Phoenix, by Deputy Sheriff Dan Nelson and W.H. Rice, a prospector who had been held up by them. But there the trail was lost, and notwithstanding the reports that the trail has been picked up again on the desert, it is now believed that the bloodthirsty outfit has made its way back to the lawless Weaver country, after visiting Phoenix in broad daylight. At Blue Tanks two nights ago, four Mexicans were on the verge of holding up a stage when they concluded it would be healthy to avoid a conflict with the passengers, and made away at a rapid gait on their Indian ponies. The driver, a young man named James Corwin, was carrying nearly $1,000 worth of bullion from the Crown King mine. As a precaution, he took a guard of five men with him over the mountains. When the stage appeared on the summit of the Crown Point mountains, the Mexicans were in a gulch, and were not long in discovering that the stage carried a formidable force. These men answered the description of those in "Pelelo's" gang, and at the point where they calculated to hold up the stage, they were within thirty miles of the Weaver district, which has afforded a safe rendezvous for them for some time.

"Pelelo," the leader of the gang, is a dare-devil with such singular luck that he is regarded by Mexicans with superstition. He has a record of killing twenty-three persons, three of whom were women, murdered by him in Chihuahua, Mexico, ten years ago, before he came to the United States. He killed a dozen Mexicans in Mexico, and has added a list of victims to his record in Arizona within a decade. He formerly congregated with his gang about Morenci, A.T., and occasionally roamed into New Mexico. His last marauding expedition in New Mexico terminated fatally for the gang. Five of the members were killed by officers at Silver City, and the four remaining returned to Morenci, where they were frequently responsible for murder until one year ago, when "Pelelo" was captured, and lingered for some time in the county jail at Morenci.

"Pelelo" was finally put in a close cell, and a death watch was maintained, but one day before the date set for his execution, which was to be a public affair, and was calculated to create much rejoicing, he broke jail and, reuniting the remnants of his gang, he has grown more ardent in crime, if possible, than ever before. The Mexicans with him were outlawed before associating themselves with him. Ramon Bluman and Federo Lucaera, two of the number, have each participated in several killings. John Stanton, who founded the town of Stanton in Central Arizona, near the Weaver district, is numbered among their victims.

As previously noted, variations on this fanciful exposé appeared in a number of newspapers across the country, including the *St. Louis Republic* on June 24, the *Star Tribune* (Minnesota) on July 1, the *El Paso Star Tribune* on July 10, the *Western Newspaper Union* (Kansas) on July 14, the *Gate City Journal* (Kansas) on July 20 and the *Parsons Daily News* (Kansas) on July 21.

As to the article itself, the author will refrain from critically dissecting it for flaws and fabrications, leaving this exercise to the discerning reader. Suffice it to say, an article that begins with so much misinformation (Juan Chacón? Really?) in the first sentence should not really be trusted as a primary, or even secondary, source document by the researcher. It is included herein only to demonstrate how utterly absurd the stories concerning Chacón activities were becoming. As hard as it might be to fathom, the stories would only become more preposterous.

Back in the Arizona Territory, it was drawing near election time, and Graham County sheriff Ben Clark had announced himself as a candidate for reelection. His challengers in the primary election were Joe T. McKinney, who had once served as undersheriff for the legendary Commodore Perry Owens of Apache County, and rancher James V. Parks. Whether he was serious in his intentions or it was just an election stunt, Sheriff Clark announced that he "in connection with other Arizona officers" was planning a raid into the vicinity of Eagle Creek for the purpose of "arresting Chacón and the gang that is supposed to be with him."

Maricopa County sheriff Murray was extremely skeptical of the success of such an operation, saying, "I do not see how any good can result from such an expedition. In the first place, there has been considerable bluster in the preparations, and as the outlaws in that county have spies in touch with the officers, they have been notified by the time that plans are being laid for this raid and had time to get away." Sheriff Murray opined further, saying that even if this posse of officers were to apprehend some of these criminals, "[t]here is positive proof again, but few of the suspicious characters whom they may find, and convictions or ability to hold them will be difficult." The lawman said that the only way to deal with such criminals and to "put a stop to the depredations of the gang" was to wait until a crime was committed, "follow the trail while it is hot, and get the men when some specific charge may be laid against them."

Word of Sheriff Clark's program was quickly and widely disseminated, as the *Fitchburg Sentinel* of Massachusetts reported on July 30 that law officers in southern Arizona were completing plans for a raid on "the murderous band of Mexicans" headquartered on Eagle Creek, as well as the Anglo-

American outlaws hiding along the Black River. The plan included the supposed use of American Indians to track the outlaws. Notice of the upcoming raid also appeared in the *Idaho Statesmen*, the *Salt Lake Tribune*, the *Inter Ocean* (Illinois), the *Oakland Tribune* and the *Wilkes-Barr Democrat*, among others.

The *Western Liberal* scoffed at Sheriff Clark's notion, saying, "It is dollars to doughnuts that Ben Clark will have a lame back again before he catches Chacón, or any of his gang [referring to the sheriff's aborted attempt to capture Chacón in August 1898]." The New Mexico newspaper declared that Chacón "goes where he pleases, and levies tribute on the Mexicans in that country. He even goes down into the railroad camps on the Morenci Southern and makes the Mexicans at work there give him grub. This they do, and do not tell of his being there until he is safe away."

This story of a coalition of officers from different counties going after Chacón and his gang soon took on a life of its own and mutated into yet another specious article that saw nationwide circulation during the first few weeks of August. Appearing in most these newspapers under the headline "A Bandit Chase," the story reads like something out of one of *Beadle's Dime Novels*. The first appearance of this story was in the August 1 edition of the *Printer*, a monthly newspaper published in Wichita, Kansas, as well as the *Stanberry Headlight* in Missouri:

A Bandit Chase
Arizona Officers and Cowboys on the War Path

Officers and cowboys from central and southern Arizona have formed the largest posse that has ever engaged in a man-hunt in the southwest and are scouring the deserts and mountain strongholds in an effort to run down the most bloodthirsty gang of stage robbers ever known to Arizona. The hunted men are four Mexicans, who ten years ago came into Arizona in great disorder from Chihuahua, Mexico, when the gang consisted of nine members, each with a remarkable criminal record. The dare-devil combination terrorized certain sections of Mexico for years, and until a whole company of Mexican gendarmes routed the Mexicans from their places of refuge in the mountains of Chihuahua and drove them out of Mexico. They found Arizona a safe place of retreat, and for a decade have been waging war against stage coaches.

In their latest rampage, they cut a wide swath from one end of the territory to the other and thoroughly aroused the settlers in their wake. Three *weeks ago, they raided a gambling house in Globe, Ariz., robbing the games of several thousand dollars. On their Indian ponies, they covered a distance of 200 miles to the Jerome mining camp in northern Arizona. Their coming was reported, and they were prevented from swooping down on the gambling houses of that place, but to compensate for the long journey they held up a miner and robbed him of $300 and escaped to the Weaver district, 150 miles distant, where a white man's life is insecure. As they started over the Crown Point mountains they came upon am old prospector named "Bill" Rice, who lived in a cabin for years and had accumulated considerable gold dust by placer digging, they fired upon the old man's cabin, but he beat them off, winging one of the bandits.*

On Their Trail

Rice went after Deputy Sheriff Dan Nelson, and the two trailed the Mexicans over the mountain divide and on to the desert south of the Crown Point mountains, reaching New River Wells, where they discovered fresh evidence of the bloody work of the desperadoes.

The dead bodies of T.W. Stewart, of Eureka, Kan., and Antone [sic] *Olsen, of Minnesota, were bleaching on the desert near the adobe house, riddles with bullets and swollen out of recognition. The two men were invalids who had not been in Arizona more than a year and were unfamiliar with the tactics employed by Arizona bandits.*

The Mexicans were trailed by Rice and Nelson to Phoenix, where the trails were lost. Posses were organized hastily and the trail was picked up a few miles from the town, but in the meantime the bandits had doubled on their trail and retraced the distance to the Crown Point mountains, baffling all pursuit. They held up a mail coach carrying eight passengers in the mountains, relieving them of their money and valuables, looting the mail pouches and securing a bar of gold bullion.

In the Superstition Mountains

When the nine Chihuahua refugees were driven from Mexico they went into the Superstition mountains in the Apache country of eastern Arizona. They were unable to make friends with the Indians, but rendezvoused near the haunts of "Bear" Reavis, an old recluse who had lived alone in the Superstition mountains for several decades, ever since he was jilted by a sweetheart in St. Louis and decided to live a life of hermitage. He lived in a cave which was festooned with the scalps of over a score of Indians, who had attempted to raid his lonely place of retirement. He was a sure shot and seldom failed to bring down an Indian when in rifle range. He boasted he never lost sight of an

> *opportunity to take the life of an Apache, and his success against roving bands of redskins, his phenomenal skill with a rifle, and the marvelous luck which repeatedly save him from the arrows of the Apache, united to strike terror to the hearts of the redskins. Eventually, they came to look upon Reavis as a supernatural being. They did not venture into the mountains within several miles of the hermit's cave, and the name "Superstition" was applied to the lonely range of mountains inhabited by no one but Reavis.*
>
> *Reavis did not make friends with the Mexican outlaw band. He was not interested in the destruction of the white race as he was in the extermination of the red race, and he did not attempt to disturb the outlaws. In turn, the Mexicans were content to find a stronghold in the mountains near him, where they were safe, not only from the vigilantes, but from the Apaches. The leader of the bandit gang, who is still heading the survivors, is Juan Chacón, commonly called "Pelelo," which, according to Mexican palaver, indicates a creature despised and feared.*

Again, this author is not going to bother with a critical evisceration of the article, as there are so many inaccuracies and so much misinformation contained within that it would require several dozen more pages and probably become quite tedious to the reader. Noteworthy, though, are the racist sentiments found within. This article, replete with these tiresome allusions, was found in more than twenty different newspapers published between August 1 and September 30 of 1900, including the *Dodge City Reporter*, the *Idaho Statesman*, the *Record-Argus* (Greenville, Pennsylvania) and the *Lead Daily Call* (South Dakota).

This does seem a good point for a discussion of Chacón's oft-employed sobriquet, "*El Peludo*." The aforementioned articles contain the first mentions in the historical record of a nickname for Chacón. It is possible that the appellation was an invention of the first author and simply reiterated by the second. It is readily apparent that neither author was bilingual (or, at least, did not speak Spanish). "Pelelo" does not exist in the Spanish language. In Spanish, "too insignificant to talk about" translates to "*demasiado insignificante para hablar de*," and the direct translation for "a creature despised and feared" is "*una criatura despreciada y temida*." It may be observed that neither of these phrases contains a word that even remotely resembles "pelelo." The word *pelo*, in Spanish, means hair. "Pelelo" means nothing at all.

Was Chacón's nickname just another creation of the media? Was the nickname "*El Peludo*" simply a modification of a nonsensical word that was invented by a hack journalist who could not speak Spanish? Or was this moniker actually employed during his lifetime by people who knew him? It is impossible to say with any authority based on the historical record. The sobriquet "*El Peludo*"—correctly spelled—would not be utilized by the newspapers for another two years. In the interim, Chacón was simply referred to in the press as "Chacón."

In regards to the much-touted raid by the law enforcement officers of Gila and Graham Counties against the bandits of Eagle Creek, the territorial newspapers reported that on July 23, Sheriff Clark and his deputies had indeed ventured into the area, with the stated intention of finding the killers of Howe and Wheeler. Was this the extent of the raid that the press, territorial and national, had written at such length about, or had Sheriff Wheeler sought to attempt a second raid, with a greater number of officers at his back? If so, it received no mentioned in the territorial newspapers. However, the *Los Angeles Times* on August 14 noted, "The raid had been started with much noise and any desperadoes in the path of the posse have had ample time in which to change location."

On August 13, after Sheriff Clark announced that he was seeking reelection, the *Western Liberal* lambasted him for his inability to capture Chacón during his tenure in office, saying, "[Sheriff Clark] probably thinks, given enough time in the office, say ten or fifteen years, he may capture the outlaw, providing the outlaw does not die of old age." In the primaries, Sheriff Clark would not even receive his party's nomination. Said nomination, and the subsequent election, would both go to James V. Parks. Parks would serve three terms as the sheriff of Graham County and be praised as one of the finest sheriffs the region ever had.[35]

THE GUTHRIE TENT-SALOON MURDERS

John McGeehan was the proprietor of a tent saloon in Guthrie, a small railroad-stop community located about twelve miles south of Clifton on the Arizona & New Mexico Railway line. McGeehan's saloon was fairly new, having been opened in April 1900. The business was located "near the Gila river," but at some remove from the station house. John McBride had moved from Clifton to Guthrie and "assisted McGeehan in his saloon business." The two men slept inside the tent when it was not open to the public.

About half past two o'clock on the morning of September 18, 1900, McGeehan's neighbors heard several gunshots, which seemed to have

Train depot in Guthrie, Arizona Territory. *Arizona Historical Society, PC 1000, Main Photo Collection, #51195.*

emanated from the saloon. They went to investigate. Upon arriving at the saloon, the neighbors were horrified to find McGeehan and McBride lying dead on the floor. Both had been shot to death. The *Graham Guardian* reported that the murderer(s) had "entered the tent by means of a hole slit in the tent with a knife." McGeehan and McBride must have been awakened by the noise and "sprang to their feet" before being gunned down. The evidence suggested that McBride had grappled with his attacker before he was killed and may well have wounded his assailant.

"A Mexican hat was found near the door," said the *Guardian*, "and the owner arrested had brought to town, and locked up by Deputy Sheriff Bell." A second man, who had been in the company of the first, was also brought in and incarcerated. McGeehan was rumored to have kept a small amount of currency and coin on hand so he could cash the checks of the workers on the Arizona & New Mexico Railway line. Additionally, he had "a number of bank checks," but these were discovered inside a locked trunk. No cash was found. It was surmised that if robbery was the motive, the assailants had escaped with very little. The *Guardian* suggested that the "gang" that committed the crime comprised three to four men. When the newspaper went to press, the names of those arrested were still being withheld pending an investigation.

The following day, the *Holbrook Argus* carried the news of the murders, adding little to the initial report found in the *Guardian* except to say that, fearing a lynching, the sheriff had stationed a guard outside the jailhouse. "[T]he following day, one of the guards, Longfellow Saldo [*sic*], was killed by a bullet from a gun carelessly handled by Manuel Bristlle, another guard." By the time the news reached San Francisco on the sixteenth (by way of the *Chronicle*), "There [was] speculation as to whether the assassination [was] the work of wood-haulers, or can be recorded as another murder for which Chacón's notorious gang of Mexicans, which infest that country, are responsible."

Allegedly, Longfellow Salcido was shot by Bristille "on account of his apparent friendship for Chacón's gang. Salcido's father, recently killed in a cutting affray, owned a mercantile establishment in Morenci, which was believed to be a 'fence' for Chacón's plunder." After the death of his father, "the son was expected to be a friend of the gang" too. When Salcido refused to receive the gang's stolen merchandise, he was marked for death. The implication was that although the death of Salcido was officially ruled an accident by a coroner's jury, Bristille was actually a hired assassin working on behalf of the Chacón gang.

The *Los Angeles Times* would make the same allegations about Chacón's involvement in the death of Longfellow Salcido, but not about his involvement in the murders of McGeehan and McBride. By the time the newspaper went to press, a man by the name of Donaciano Corona had been charged with the homicides. While the territorial newspapers provided scant information, the October 21 edition of the *Times* reported Corona's arrest, calling the spectacle of his wife showing up at the depot in Clifton "pathetic." Mrs. Felicia Corona, described as "an ignorant young woman with a babe in arms," allegedly said that "now that her husband was going, she did not know where to turn for bread, and asked to be taken with her husband to jail, where she would at least be fed."

Donaciano Corona was tried in the district court on October 22 before Justice Fletcher Doan. Mr. Corona was represented by F.B. Laine. The prosecution called Charles Schaeffer, Huan Fierro and E.M. Williams as witnesses. The defense relied on Donaciano Corona and his wife. "The jury remained out all night, and finally brought in a verdict of murder in the second degree." The defendant was sentenced to twenty years by Justice Doan. On October 25, 1900, Donaciano Corona was received at the Yuma Territorial Prison and given inmate no. 1687. What became of Mrs. Corona and her child remains unknown.

The revolting display of racist stereotyping by the reporter from the *Los Angeles Times* in regard to Mrs. Corona aside, it can be seen once again how Chacón, and/or some member of the gang he was alleged to be leading, was continually being involved, sometimes in the most peripheral manner, by the territorial and/or the national press in any crime that was perpetrated by a person of Hispanic background in the Arizona Territory. Even when there would seem to be no possible way to connect Chacón to a specific crime, or when a crime could have been committed by virtually anyone in the territory, somehow, in some way, the press would still default to Chacón as the prime suspect.[36]

The Headless Corpse

In late November, when the decomposing, decapitated corpse of an unknown man was discovered "between the Coronado stage station and Guthrie" in Graham County, with a bullet hole in the side for good measure, the crime was immediately laid at Chacón's feet by the newspapers. The dead man was reportedly Hispanic and, therefore, classed as a criminal of some stripe. Further, he was purported to be part of the "gang led by Chacón" that had robbed and killed McGeehan and McBride in their tent saloon, even though, six weeks prior, Donaciano Corona was also said to be part of the gang. The press concluded that the man had been killed because he had been badly wounded during the robbery and could not ride, or perhaps he had been "butchered in a fight over the distribution of the booty."

This murder could have been committed by anyone in the territory, but Augustine Chacón still received the blame.

The year 1900 ended without any further news of Chacón, but there was mention of two of his alleged gang members, Juan Hernandez and Jesus Lerma, in the *San Francisco Chronicle* on December 9. Hernandez and Lerma—described by a reporter, who had never seen either of them, as "two tough-looking Mexicans"—had been arrested and charged with "complicity" in the McGeehan and McBride homicides. They were reportedly held in the county jail in Solomonville, but due to a lack of hard evidence, the pair had been released from custody.

"The officers are positive they had two members of Juan Chacón's famous gang of bandits," wrote the reporter, "which was almost certainly responsible for the sensational double killing." Upon their release, it was alleged that Hernandez and Lerma had started back toward the Eagle Creek with the intention of joining back up with the gang. The *Holbrook Argus*, which also briefly reported on the release of Hernandez and Lerma in its December 15 edition, said, "[I]t is generally believed the two Mexicans were guilty, but no convicting evidence could be obtained."

This statement from the editor of the *Argus*, with its presumption of guilt, could very well be applied to the fantastic mythology that has enveloped the person of Augustine Chacón.[37]

CHAPTER 6

BETRAYED TO THE LAW

It is not known when Augustine Chacón befriended Albert Wright "Burt" Alvord, who was previously mentioned in his role as a Cochise County deputy sheriff, working under Sheriff John Slaughter. Alvord also served as a deputy sheriff/constable in Willcox, having been appointed to that position by Cochise County sheriff Scott White. In December 1899, Alvord quit his job in law enforcement, allegedly due to ongoing disunity between himself and his boss. It was rumored that Alvord was abusing his power and taking advantage of his position as a law officer to enrich himself and his cronies, and Sheriff White did not approve.

Neither Sheriff White nor Augustine Chacón had any inclination as to how duplicitous Burt Alvord could actually be, but in time, they would both find out.

The first mention Chacón received in a territorial newspaper in 1901 was in connection with the arrest of Cornelius Pesquera by former sheriff Scott White in Naco, a town located about twelve miles to the south of Bisbee, which straddles the border between the United States and Mexico. The *Cochise Review* reported the incident on January 19, stating that Pesquera was "the man who killed two or three Mexicans in the Dragoons several months ago" and subsequently escaped into Sonora. Additionally, the suspect was said to be "partner of the noted outlaw Augustin Chacón." The newspaper supplied no details regarding his alleged crimes or his apprehension, saying only that Pesquera had been recognized by the ex-sheriff, taken into custody and transported to the jail in Tombstone.

Left: Albert Wright "Burt" Alvord. *Arizona Historical Society, PC 1000, Main Photo Collection, #20596.*

Below: The town of Naco, Arizona Territory. *Arizona Historical Society, PC 1000, Main Photo Collection, #28401.*

Cornelius Pesquera's name only appears in the territorial newspapers in connection with this arrest. His name does not appear in the Arizona Department of Corrections historical register of inmates, so it may be assumed that he was never convicted of this crime. Further, this author, searching back over two years, was unable to find any record of two or three "Mexicans" being killed in the Dragoon Mountains or any prior mention of a Cornelius Pesquera (or variations on this name). This is not to say that Pesquera was not a murderer—only that there is no supporting evidence for the allegation made by the reporter. As has been previously shown, this predilection for fabricating tall tales about suspects, especially those of Hispanic descent, appears to have been a commonplace practice in the territorial press.

Curiously, this particular news item garnered national attention and was subsequently disseminated to dozens of towns and cities across the country, including St. Joseph, Odgen, Topeka, San Francisco, Los Angeles (the *Times*, always prone to exaggeration, accused Pesquera of killing a "score of men"), El Paso and Nashville. Never one to let a popular story simply fade, the *San Francisco Chronicle* announced on January 27 that Chacón and his gang were planning to raid Tombstone and break Pesquera out of jail. Chacón, the newspaper stated, "is the leader of the most desperate gang of outlaws in the Southwest, who has many murders charged against him, and who has time and again been cornered by officers and fought his way clear, until it is said by the Mexicans that he leads a charmed life."

Chacón, it was said, "can easily muster a band of two score or more from among the Mexican wood-choppers," whom the newspaper, in all seriousness, stated were "among the most desperate characters in the world." This most dire of predictions was also given mention in the *San Francisco Call* and the *Los Angeles Times*, but without the attendant detail that the *Chronicle* had added to the story. Of course, the Tombstone raid never materialized, and Chacón disappeared for about three months from the territorial press.[38]

The Key Personages

Here is where the story begins to become a bit confusing, as there are as many different versions of it as there are people involved (more, in fact, as one of these individuals kept changing his version of the story). Let us meet them.

The town of Cochise, Arizona Territory. *Sulphur Springs Valley Historical Society, Willcox, Arizona (Sanders Family Collection).*

First there is Augustine Chacón, whom you, the reader, are already acquainted with.

Second, the aforementioned Albert "Burt" Alvord, who as it turned out was playing on both sides of the law. While still employed as a deputy sheriff, Alvord and several of his saloon buddies in Willcox planned the robbery of the westbound Southern & Pacific No. 10 train, at the depot, in the small community of Cochise, located about thirty miles east of Benson. On September 19, 1899, while the train was idling at the station, two armed, masked men took the train crew hostage and uncoupled the locomotive, tender and express car from the rest of the train. These they moved about a mile and a half down the track. Once there, the bandits opened the express car, dynamited the iron safe inside and cleaned it out.

Express companies of this era, like Wells, Fargo and Company, the company whose car was robbed in Cochise, were extremely reticent concerning how much was lost in a robbery. However, the *Oasis* newspaper estimated that the bandits' haul was between $5,000 and $30,000. Needless to say, Alvord, who was later implicated as the mastermind behind the Cochise heist, and his partners in crime were well-pleased with the end results of their foray into the business of train robbery, so much so that the gang decided to attempt it again five months later. That turned out to be a very big mistake.

According to *The Tombstone Epitaph*, it was about 6:10 p.m. on February 15, 1901, when the New Mexico and Arizona northbound No. 10 pulled into the station at Fairbank, a town located about nine miles from Tombstone, the county seat. The platform was teeming with passengers, freighters and train men when the six bandits made their entrance, firing their pistols in the air in an attempt to cow the crowd. Once the people who were occupying the railway platform were lined up, with their hands pointing skyward, the outlaws approached the express car. What exactly happened next has been debated by Old West aficionados for more than one hundred years.

Suffice it to say, a firefight erupted between the express messenger, a tough former Texas Ranger named Jefferson Davis "Jeff" Milton, and the bandits. During the melee, one of the outlaws, Jesse "Three-Finger Jack" Dunlap, was mortally wounded, his bowels perforated with buckshot, and Milton was shot thorough the arm. Their plans having been foiled by Milton, the outlaws quickly departed. Out on the trail, Dunlap, too weak to ride, tumbled from his horse and was left behind by his confederates. The following day, the unfortunate outlaw was found by a sheriff's posse, arrested and taken back to Tombstone. Within the space of a few weeks, the entire gang was captured and incarcerated, including Burt Alvord and William Downing, two of the three men who masterminded the robbery.

Third in this cast of characters is William Larkin "Billy" Stiles, who was undoubtedly one of the shrewdest outlaws to ever grace the territory. It has long been assumed that "Three-Finger Jack" Dunlap, as he lay dying in the hospital in Tombstone, gave up his pals in revenge for their leaving him behind. In fact, it was Billy Stiles who betrayed the gang to the authorities in an effort to keep himself out of jail. Conversely, it was also Stiles who walked casually into the Cochise County Jail, on the ground floor of the Tombstone Courthouse, on April 7, shot the jailor in the leg and freed Burt Alvord and John "Bravo Juan" Yoas, one of the other suspected Fairbanks robbers.

Stiles, who had admitted to authorities that he was one of the two men who had robbed the train at Cochise; Alvord, who was Stiles's close friend; and Yoas went on the lam for about two months. Then, in July, in a most surprising turn of events, Stiles surrendered to the Cochise County authorities. The timing was fortuitous, to say the least. Stiles, as he had promised, testified against all the robbers and co-conspirator William Downing in both the territorial and federal cases, which resulted in the convictions of all the principals in the Fairbanks robbery—all except Alvord and Yoas, who remained on the lam. Stiles's testimony also resulted in all the indictments against him being dropped by the territorial and federal prosecutors.

Billy Stiles, for all intents and purposes, was a free man, but his best friend, Burt Alvord, was still a fugitive from justice. Stiles, in what may strike one as

Burton Mossman, the first captain of the Arizona Rangers

Top, left: Jefferson Davis "Jeff" Milton, Wells, Fargo Express Messenger. *Private collection.*

Top, right: Jesse "Three-Finger Jack" Dunlap. *Pinal County Historical Society.*

Bottom, right: William Larkin "Billy" Stiles. *Arizona Historical Society, PC 1000, Main Photo Collection, #20586.*

Bottom, left: Captain Burton C. "Burt" Mossman. Portrait as it appeared in *Pearson's Magazine* (1905). *Author's collection.*

a strange display of fidelity considering his history with Alvord, felt obliged to do something about this.

The last in this cast of characters is Burton Charles "Burt" Mossman, who had previously been employed as the superintendent for the Aztec Land and Cattle Company, better known as "The Hashknife." Owing to his experience in hunting down and the capturing cattle rustlers, thirty-three-year-old Mossman had been appointed as the first captain of the Arizona Rangers. The Arizona Rangers, authorized in March 1901 by the Twenty-First Territorial Legislature, were a paramilitary law enforcement body with jurisdiction throughout the territory. Although the organization lasted only seven years, many modern historians have credited the Arizona Rangers with helping to curtail crime in the southern Arizona Territory. Certainly they were instrumental in this process.[39]

The Warren Ranch Heist

On March 9, 1901, the *Cochise Review* reported that Alvord, who was still a fugitive, had, on the previous Sunday, paid an unannounced visit to the Warren Ranch in the Sulphur Springs Valley, near the town of Pearce. Not wanting to appear ungracious, Frank Swink and his wife, who were the only ones at the ranch at the time, invited Alvord and his companion, initially described by the newspapers as "a Yaqui Indian," inside. Saying that he was hungry, Alvord demanded dinner from his hosts, who quickly served him. Alvord and the "Yaqui Indian" ate their meal "with their Winchesters across their laps." After they had enjoyed their repast, Alvord and his companion departed, but not before warning Mr. Swink "not to leave the place or divulge their whereabouts."

The following evening, Alvord and his companion returned to the Warren Ranch and imposed on their hosts to cook them yet another meal. Alvord seemed more at ease on this second visit to the Swinks', eating leisurely and "chatting about his experiences and how he had evaded the officers." Alvord decided to impose further on Swink's hospitality and asked that sleeping arrangements be made for himself and his friend. This was done, and the dubious guests of the house, and their cordial hosts, retired to their slumbers. Alvord and his companion slept but a short time, arose and made ready to take their leave of the Swinks. Mr. Swink was again warned "to remain in the house" and not do anything foolish.

Cochise County sheriff Adelbert V. "Del" Lewis. *Arizona State Library Archives & Public Records, History and Archives Division, Phoenix, #98-0491.*

The next morning, Mr. Swink discovered that "the recipients of his hospitality showed their ingratitude by taking five horses from the ranch," two of which belonged to Swink himself. The theft of his horses drove Swink to action. He hastened to Pearce, where he reported to the authorities the details of Alvord's visits and the theft. Mr. Swink subsequently joined the posse that was hastily assembled to track the thieves. After receipt of a telegram from Pearce, Cochise County sheriff Adelbert V. "Del" Lewis, who had succeeded Scott White, formed a posse of his own and headed out toward the Dragoon Mountains—a known haven for fugitives. A third posse was organized by Deputy Sheriff Porter McDonald and headed out to the south, in the hopes of cutting Alvord off before he could cross back in to Mexico.

"The whereabouts of Burt Alvord," wrote a columnist for the *Republican* on March 14, "has assumed another phase in the fact reports from different sections of the county, all positively claiming that the noted outlaw has been seen at these various places, indicate that Alvord is riding over considerable country, and evidently has some mischievous purpose in mind." *The Epitaph* reported on March 17 that nothing had been heard from any of the three indefatigable posses, but that the officers were still afield in search of the outlaws.[40] Certainly no one—neither the law officers nor the press—expected what the next notices concerning Alvord would reveal.

On March 29, 1901, a reporter from the *Arizona Daily Star* received a telephone message from Alvan W. Howe, ex-editor of the *Arizona Orb*, informing him that just the evening before, Alvord and two companions had ridden into Douglas, a town of about four thousand inhabitants, located on the northern side of the United States–Mexico border, and had brazenly visited several saloons in that burg, drinking and carousing until early hours of the morning. The Cochise County officers were immediately notified by telegraph of this most recent sighting of Alvord, and another sheriff's posse was dispatched from Tombstone. The *Daily Star* reasoned, "As the outlaws have only a few hours start, a battle may be looked forward to."

What came as a surprise was the affirmation that one of the men who had accompanied Alvord on his visit to Douglas had been identified by "a

The town of Douglas, Arizona Territory. *Arizona Historical Society, PC 191, Douglas Photographs, Box 1, Folder 1, #B.*

Mexican bartender" as none other than Augustine Chacón. The saloon man said he had known Chacón in Clifton and had had the opportunity to talk with him briefly when he came into the saloon in Douglas with Alvord. *The Epitaph* said that Chacón had also been with Alvord "when he had the raid at Pearce," referring to the theft of the five horses from the Warren Ranch. The posse that had been dispatched from Tombstone was able to locate the outlaws' camp outside of Douglas and, when last heard from, were hot on the trail. Alas, this pursuit would also be in vain.

The news that Chacón and Alvord were riding together was subsequently verified by "a Mexican woodcutter" who had visited Bisbee the week before. The woodcutter told the authorities that Chacón, Alvord and a third man had visited his camp the previous Monday, March 25, and had dinner with him. The man stated that the three outlaws "had four horses and were heavily armed." The woodcutter did not know the identity of the third man in the party but said that the trio left immediately after dinner, riding along the canyon, and appeared to be headed off to the south toward the international border.

Oddly, the news of the alliance of these two noted bandits, both of whom had garnered their fair share of press, seemed of little interest to the newspaper editors. The only publications that made mention of this apparent partnering of Alvord and Chacón inside the territory were *The*

Tombstone Epitaph, the *Bisbee Review*, the *Arizona Journal-Miner* and the *Florence Tribune*, while outside the territory, except for the briefest of mentions in the *El Paso Herald*, the *San Bernardino Transcript* and the *Albuquerque Journal*, the news was virtually ignored.

The *Graham Guardian* reported that on May 3, a posse, led by Safford City marshal A.A. McKinzie and consisting of himself and six others, had departed from Solomonville and ridden out in the direction of Clifton; a second posse, led by Sheriff James Parks, had departed Clifton, heading in the direction of Safford. "The reason of these movements is that on Tuesday [April 30], a Mexican came in and informed Sheriff Parks that Chacón, the murderer of Pabalo [*sic*] Salcido, and his gang were camped in the mountains near Gutherie [*sic*] and that he would lead them to the place." The posses were dutifully organized and an expedition undertaken, but Chacón was not found. The newspaper said, "[T]here was little doubt as to the authenticity of the information given by the Mexican," so it was assumed that Chacón had been tipped off and skinned out. Of course, the real reason Chacón was not found by the posses was because he was south of the border keeping company with Burt Alvord.[41]

While Burt Alvord continued to receive notice in the press throughout 1901—being seen in Sonora in early July; being said to have robbed a monte game (monte was a popular frontier gambling game, though rarely played today) in Naco with one Sidney Johnson later the same month; being killed while attempting to rob a messenger of the Sonora Mining Company in Tubutana in November (he wasn't); and being killed again in a "three-cornered duel" by a "nervy killer" (and, again, he wasn't)—Chacón appears to have been completely forgotten by the press, both territorially and nationally, until January of the following year.[42]

Under the headline "Doom of Arizona Bandits," the *El Paso Times* unabashedly praised the "stringent law" passed by the Arizona Territorial Legislature in March 1901 that empowered Governor Oakes Murphy to "organize a company of rangers whose especial [*sic*] business it shall be to run the robbers to cover and, if they cannot be taken alive, to kill them like so many wild beasts." Burt Mossman was designated as the captain of this elite law enforcement unit, and he personally had made "a careful selection of the most intrepid men" to complete his force. The *Times* stated that the Arizona Rangers had been afield since August of the previous year, "scouring plains and mountain strongholds for desperadoes."

Meanwhile, reported the El Paso newspaper, President José de la Cruz Porfirio Díaz Mori of Mexico had ordered Colonel Emilio Kosterlitzky

Left: President José de la Cruz Porfirio Díaz Mori of Mexico. *Library of Congress.*

Right: Colonel Emilio Kosterlitzky. *Library of Congress.*

and *La Gendarmería Fiscal*, better known in the United States simply as the *Rurales*, "to patrol the border with increased vigor, and lend all possible assistance to the rangers in ridding the international border of common enemies." To this end, Captain Mossman and Colonel Kosterlitzky met in Bisbee to discuss a strategy for their "co-operative war on all refugees." The newspaper reported that "official recognition of the understanding between the two countries" occurred when Territorial Governor Murphy sent Sonoran governor Rafael Izabal a requisition for a suspected Yuma murderer, which was honored by Governor Izabal, after he received a directive directly from President Díaz, instructing him "to waive unnecessary formality in delivering" the suspect to the territorial authorities.

Colonel Kosterlitzky, a former Russian navy midshipman who deserted in Venezuela and subsequently joined the Mexican army, was afforded a brief biography in the article. Kosterlitzky was portrayed as a man absolutely devoid of fear and empathy. "The colonel is vested with the power not only of a military officer, but of a tribunal. It is not infrequent for him to capture a criminal, sit in expeditious trial over him, and witness his expiation at the end of a riata, all before breakfast. Such is the wrath of the gendarmes against the 'bad man,' nor does the government frown at that kind of quick retribution," the author said admiringly.

Burt Alvord was specifically named in the *Times* article. It was stated that he and his confederates had "laughed at the former efforts of officers and vigilantes to shake them from their strongholds" and revealed how Alvord amused himself by sending taunting letters to sheriffs, telling them where in the mountains he and his band were located, inviting their pursuit and "promising the officers, in a jocular way, that they would give them a warm reception." The *Times* asserted that in going in pursuit of bandits and outlaws like Alvord, the Rangers had undertaken a most difficult and dangerous mission, one that already had cost the lives of two of their number.

Augustine Chacón, who was again referred to by the meaningless nickname of "Pelelo," was also given mention in the column as being the leader of an infamous gang and having twenty-eight murders to his credit. "[T]he list would be much greater if all his victims were known," asserted the article's author. The nameless "vaqueros" who comprised the balance of Chacón's gang were said to have criminal records just as "startling" as Chacón's. It was further stated that the "Mexican Rurales" had taken a special interest in bringing down the lot of them.

The *El Paso Times* concluded its aggrandizing exposé about Captain Mossman and the Arizona Rangers by saying, "The people of the

La Gendarmería Fiscal, or the *Rurales*. *Private collection.*

southwest heartily approve of the energy displayed in the direction of the suppression of outlawry, and look forward to the day, not far distant they hope, when that region will be as safe for the traveler to traverse as any portion of the United States."

The next mention of Chacón's name in a territorial newspaper came on February 1, 1902, when the *Tucson Citizen* reported that Graham County sheriff James Parks had met with Captain Mossman of the Arizona Rangers to discuss "the best means to capture Augustin Chacón, the famous murderer, who is wanted in Graham county, as well as every other county in the Territory." The article accused Chacón of killing seven men in the New River section and proclaimed that there was a $5,000 bounty on his head (there was not). Although the newspaper refrained from saying that he was the leader, Chacón was suspected of having recently "joined a band of cattle thieves." It was further stated that the outlaw resided in "the mountains" when he not out committing crimes. Chacón's association with Alvord was not mentioned.

Alvord was next reported having been sighted in the town of Cananea, Sonora, "in the vicinity of the Puertecitas Mine," with a Mexican partner, who was alleged to be "Bravo Juan" Yoas, the Fairbanks train robber who, it will be remembered, had escaped with Alvord from the Tombstone jail. However, the "Mexican partner" may well have been Chacón, although this cannot be verified either way. It was stated in the *Bisbee Daily Review* that Alvord, who was described as wearing a "heavy beard," and "his Mexican partner" had visited Proetor's Saloon for a drink and some roulette. Alvord was said to have won forty dollars at the table.

It was suggested by the author of the article that Alvord was "hovering around" Cananea because Billy Stiles was employed there as a driver on an ore wagon at the Puertecitas mine. Alvord, it was said, intended to kill Stiles for turning state's evidence against him. This would by completely understandable and even plausible, Alvord having murdered at least one man in his lifetime (a cowboy named William "Bill" King in Willcox, purportedly in retaliation for a practical joke). But did Alvord truly want to kill Stiles, or had he an ulterior motive for remaining in the vicinity of Cananea? Later developments would suggest that the fugitive indeed had something else in mind.

Five days later, the *Daily Review* amended this report, stating that "Bravo Juan" Yoas was "not a Mexican, as the name would indicate," but an Anglo named "John Yast." This lends some credence to the supposition that it was actually Chacón who had been with Alvord in Proetor's Saloon, since the

Graham County sheriff James V. Jim Parks. *Arizona Historical Society, PC 161, Ringgold Photo Collection, Box 1, Folder 1, #J.*

man was decidedly described as being "Mexican." Granted, it could well have been another gentleman of Hispanic heritage.[43]

While Mossman and his Rangers were busy chasing after Alvord, Chacón and some of the lesser luminaries in the outlaw pantheon in and around Cochise County, Sheriff James Parks was occupied with the task of cleaning up his own backyard, so to speak. In April, the *Western Liberal* reported that the lawman and a posse of five had ventured up on Eagle Creek with the stated intention of routing "the Chacón gang of Mexican outlaws." The gang was suspected of having recently rustled five head of cattle from Benjamin Parks (of no relation).

Early on the morning of April 7, 1902, the posse quietly slipped up and surrounded the stone house the suspects were inhabiting. Although he had five men to back his play, Sheriff Parks entered the domicile alone, "his only arms being a sixshooter [*sic*] which was in his pocket." He was met by one Manuel Martinez, who was armed with a Winchester rifle. Martinez proceeded to raise the rifle and point it in the sheriff's direction, but before the outlaw could squeeze the trigger, Sheriff Parks pulled his pistol and shot Martinez. Martinez fell to the floor, fatally wounded, and died within a few minutes.

Upon seeing what had become of their *compadré*, the other two inhabitants of the house decided that it would be inadvisable to resist the officers and submitted to arrest. A short while later, four more men rode onto the property, and they, too, were arrested. This was accomplished without another shot being fired. The suspects—identified by the *Arizona Sentinel* as Simon Antonia, Martin Santana, Felicio Martinez, Francisco Florez, Lucera Herrera and Valente Parra—were transported to Solomonville, where they were jailed.

As might well be expected, the *Lordsburg Liberal* accused the apprehended men of several killings but neglected to give any specifics concerning these murders, such as who the victims were or where the killings had occurred. The *Liberal* added, "[T]he notorious Chacón, who escaped from the Solomonville jail while under sentence of death, has been with the gang, and is supposed to be the leader of them, but, unfortunately, was away at the time Sheriff Parks called." Of course, Chacón was most likely in Mexico, where he had been residing for some time. Still, the New Mexico newspaper praised Sheriff Parks as "the best sheriff Graham county ever had."[44]

"The character that is most wanted by the Rangers…[and] must soon yield to the law is Augustin Chacón, known as Chacón, the most notorious outlaw who ever led a band of lawless characters," declared Captain Mossman in an interview with the *Bisbee Daily Review*, published on April 27. "Chacón," it was reported, was "part Mexican, containing all the characteristice [*sic*] of the race and possessing at the same time a rare degree of native ability, which is all concentrated in carrying out his reckless and nefarious deeds." It would seem that Chacón was becoming so distinguished in his infamy, and so adept at outwitting the officers who sought him, that he had almost managed to transcend the racist stereotypes reserved by Anglos, like the *Daily Review* editor William Kelly, for persons of Hispanic heritage.

In what had by this time become the standard litany in the articles about Chacón, he was said to have lived a life "checkered with murder," commanded a gang comprising some of the most "noted bandits of Arizona and New Mexico" and stolen cattle and horses in "great numbers." His escape from the Solomonville jail was also mentioned. However, the death of Pablo Salcido was completely omitted. The *Daily Review* erroneously asserted that Chacón had "committed murder in two or three instances in the most cold-blooded form," and it was these murders that had led to his being "arrested, tried, convicted, and sentenced to hang." Most recently, reported the *Daily Review*, "he has been on this side of the line, and drove a herd of horses into Mexico."

With the self-serving braggadocio that would mark his later interviews, Captain Mossman said, "This desperado is especially desired by officers. When he is apprehended, the acknowledged leader of the robber bands will be out of the way, and it will tend to break up the gangs. We will hunt this man down and bring him to justice." In the light of how Chacón would finally be captured, this last statement is especially incongruous.

This article was reprinted word for word in the *Arizona Daily Star* three days later. On the same day, in the *Daily Review*, Sheriff Lewis of Cochise County shared his opinions about Burt Alvord and the likelihood of his capture. "I think Alvord is somewhere near Cananea, and may, at times, come close to the mining camp," the lawman was quoted as saying. "To catch this noted outlaw is a difficult matter, and, as long as he keeps with people of his own kind, the officers will have a big job on their hands. Alvord knows the country and can depend on certain Mexicans to help

First Company Arizona Rangers, circa 1901. *Private collection.*

him should he get in a tight pinch. If he should be caught, a hard fight would have to be made to get him out of the country." This statement would also prove to be ironic.

"Has Killed Forty-Two Men" was the headline most of the national newspapers utilized for a small item about Chacón, first published in the *San Francisco Examiner*. The article, which ran to only two short paragraphs, was an amalgamation of the longer articles that appeared previously in the *El Paso Times* and the *Bisbee Daily Review*. The *Examiner* proclaimed that Captain Mossman and his Arizona Rangers, as well as Colonel Kosterlitzky and his gendarmes, had combined forces "to run to death that most blood-thirsty of all Mexican bandits, Augustin Chacón."

If the item in the *Examiner* was to be believed, Chacón had "terrorized" the border for a "generation," "committing murder after murder, and escaping with seemingly superhuman skill." Although the newspaper did not provide the source for the quote, it reported that Chacón boasted of killing forty-two men. Mossman, who was wrongly credited by the paper with breaking up the "Musegrave gang," also known as the High-Five Gang, asserted that with "the capture or death of Chacón," banditry along the border would come to an end. This report from the *Examiner* was disseminated by the wire service to newspapers across the country, including those in Kansas, Utah, Mississippi, Pittsburgh, Wisconsin and Montana.[45]

Then, for almost three months, nothing more was reported about either Chacón or Alvord.

The Media Version

The month of September 1902 began with the most astonishing news. Augustine Chacón, "the noted Mexican murderer and all-around bandit," had finally been apprehended on the San Pedro River, near the town of Hereford, by Captain Mossman of the Arizona Rangers, working in conjunction with Billy Stiles. The *Copper Era* and the *Tucson Citizen* were the first newspapers to report on this most unanticipated capture. The latter referred to the fugitive by the name "Juan Chacón," with the balance of its exclusive, detailing his alleged crimes and capture, being equally inaccurate. The former mistakenly credited Sheriff James Parks with the apprehension of "the noted outlaw and highwaymen."

The *Arizona Republican*, the *Arizona Daily Star* and the *Bisbee Daily Review* reported the news the following day. "This capture is a very important one," the *Daily Star* informed its readers, "as Chacón has been a much-wanted man for the last four years, when he escaped from Solomonville jail, where he was under sentence of death for a most brutal murder committed in Morenci." The Tucson newspaper went on to accuse Chacón of the murders of six other persons as well as "numerous petty offences." the *Republican* also accused Chacón of committing a "half a dozen murders" and spuriously stated that he had incurred the death penalty for murdering a woman in Clifton six years prior.

How the capture of Chacón was orchestrated, who exactly was involved and what their involvement was remains unclear. The first comprehensive report about Chacón's arrest came from the *Bisbee Daily Review*, which credited Captain Burt Mossman with "the capture of this noted outlaw, who has been the terror of Graham and Cochise counties for the last five years." The apprehension was said to have been "the culmination of a deep laid plan."

Burt Mossman had officially resigned from the Arizona Rangers on September 1, 1902, but received word on Tuesday, September 2, from an undisclosed source that Chacón intended to raid the horse pasture at the Sneed Ranch, seven miles north of the international border that very evening. Mossman, in the company of Billy Stiles, immediately left for that part of the country. Upon arriving at their destination, the two men staked out the ranch. Unfortunately, Chacón never appeared, and their "vigilance was unrewarded."

Still, the two officers were not to be deterred, and after spending the day at a nearby ranch, they resumed their stakeout on Wednesday evening. "They did not have long to wait, for about 11 o'clok [*sic*], a horseman rode into a small canyon nearby" and set up his camp. It was Chacón. Mossman reasoned that since the sky was overcast and it was quite dark out, Chacón would wait for daylight to rustle the horses. The first incongruity one finds in this version of the story is an explanation of how Mossman and Stiles managed to recognize the horseman as Chacón on such a dark and gloomy night, especially when neither was previously acquainted with the man.

The ex-captain and Stiles, with the most admirable stealth, crept up on Chacón while he was in his camp, found position and waited until "the first peep of day." On Thursday, as dawn was breaking across the Sonoran Desert, Mossman called out to Chacón in Spanish and ordered him to "throw up his hands" and surrender. "Mossman was close beside him when the command was given, and had him covered. Stiles was on the other side of the outlaw, ready to shoot him if he made a move."

Herein lies the second fault with this version: How did Mossman and Stiles manage to get so close to Chacón, unless he was fast asleep or preoccupied? Typically, a man about to commit a crime is extremely cognizant of his surroundings, and it would seem that Chacón, being the shrewd and cunning criminal he was purported to be, would have noticed the two officers long before they were "close beside him." The whole scenario of Mossman and Stiles sneaking up on Chacón like ninjas can only be regarded as being highly implausible.

"Chacón," said the newspaper, "did not get rattled. He had long ago learned to hold his nerve in check in the face of danger. He looked up in the face of Mossman, his brows contracted lightly, those black eyes on his captor, said in Spanish, '*Mátame. ¿Por qué no sigues y me matas? Sé que me matarás.*' [Kill me. Why don't you go ahead and kill me? I know you will kill me.]" Not understanding what Chacón was attempting to communicate—that he would probably have preferred to be shot to death than to be hanged or incarcerated in Yuma for life—Mossman promised Chacón that no harm would come to him "if he would come along peaceably." The former Ranger then ordered Stiles to disarm their captive. Stiles relieved Chacón of his cartridge belt, from which hung a holstered pistol and a bowie knife, and handcuffed Chacón's wrists together.

With Chacón secured, the horses were saddled, and the trio began the ride to the train station in Naco, with Mossman taking the lead, Stiles bringing up the rear and Chacón positioned betwixt them. Once the party reached Naco, they boarded the train for Benson. In Benson, they were met by Sheriff Parks, who had been "advised Chacón would soon be in the hands of the officers." Mossman turned Chacón over to Sheriff Parks to be escorted back to Solomonville. While the lawman and Chacón were waiting at the Benson station for the train, a reporter from the *Daily Review* asked permission to speak with Sheriff Park's prisoner. This favor was granted the newspaperman.

"The Mexican outlaw, who does not know the meaning of fear, took his capture philosophically," said the reporter.

"Where are you going, Chacón?"

"I suppose they are taking me to Solomonville," replied Chacón, "and I want them to kill me this time. I prefer death to a term in the penitentiary." It wasn't much of an interview, possibly because of the language barrier between the reporter and the outlaw.

Train depot, Benson, Arizona Territory. *Arizona Post Offices Photograph Collection, PC001, Postal History Foundation.*

The newspaperman observed that Chacón had "broken rapidly" in the five years since his escape. "His form is bent and his beard in tinged with gray. To be hunted like an animal for five years has left its mark on the outlaw." The newspaper ended the report on the capture of Chacón with congratulations being proffered to ex-captain Mossman and Billy Stiles on their "daring undertaking and its successful culmination."[46]

When it is asserted that Mossman voluntarily resigned his position with the Arizona Rangers, it is equivocation. In fact, he gave up the position because, on August 18, a petition was circulated in Bisbee, signed by more than fifty citizens, calling on Governor Alexander Oswald Brodie to "immediately remove from his present position as captain in the Arizona rangers…Burton C. Mossmann [*sic*]." The author of the petition said that it had "become evident, from a number of disgraceful transactions that have occurred in our midst of late…the captain is a disgrace to the office that he holds, and a menace to this community."

Said petition was circulated in reaction to an incident that occurred during the early morning hours of Saturday, August 16, at the Orient Saloon. Ranger Burt Grover had an altercation over a poker game with a local gambler named Daniel "Dan" Callaghan whom Grover accused of cheating. During the argument, Grover allegedly drew his weapon. When he realized what was occurring, Captain Mossman stepped in "to quiet Grover" and, with help from Ranger Leonard Page, was able to steer Grover away from Callaghan.

At about this time, city police officers Harold "Harry" Jennings and James Harrington arrived on the scene, and moments later, the two police officers and the three Rangers were "scuffling." The brawl spilled out into the street, but no one was severely injured. During the melee, Officer Harrington managed to secure Grover's pistol and subsequently placed him under arrest for "disturbing the peace." Grover was taken to jail.

Territorial Governor Alexander Oswald Brodie. *Arizona State Library Archives & Public Records, History and Archives Division, Phoenix, #97-8064.*

Later that afternoon, "Ranger Page secured the keys to the jail, from the office of [Justice of the Peace] S.K. Williams, and liberated Grover." When the jail delivery was discovered, the city police officers swore out a warrant against Leonard Page as well. However, they were unable to serve said warrant, as Ranger Page and Ranger Grover had skipped town.

Realizing that this altercation with local law enforcement reflected very poorly on the Rangers and him personally, Captain Mossman went to the newspaper in an attempt to clear the incident up. Mossman stated, "Ranger Grover had a difficulty with a gambler" and "some words were passed." However, Mossman said, Grover was not really to blame, as he had been "in a boisterous mood" (i.e., inebriated). Mossman further declared that it was he who had arrested Grover and that Officers Harrington and Jennings had only aided him in disarming Grover. Somehow, this process of disarming Ranger Grover had resulted in the lot of them falling "through the front door the Orient and out on to the street." The captain said nothing about the jail delivery.

Unfortunately for Mossman, his whitewashing of the incident at the Oriental was too little, too late. The public was incensed at the liberties taken by the captain and his Rangers and demanded his immediate dismissal. However, rather than let it look as though he had been forced from office by this public outcry, Mossman sent a telegram to the offices of the *Bisbee Daily Review*, asserting that he had tendered his resignation by letter to Governor Brodie back in July and expected that said resignation would be accepted by August 31, 1902.

The Bisbee newspaper reported, "When Governor Brodie assumed office, the resignation was placed in his hands, but owing to a secret piece of detective work, which the Rangers had at hand, [it] was not accepted." On August 21, Governor Brodie, for reasons undisclosed, decided to go along with the lawman's subterfuge, sending a letter to Mossman, in reply to his earlier missive, stating that he would officially accept the captain's resignation on September 1, 1902.

This account of the resignation of Captain Mossman may well be true, but the fact that Mossman did not give a reason for his decision to resign in his letter to the governor makes the predated resignation announcement seem like a contrivance. Additionally, it makes Mossman's subsequent capture of Chacón appear all the more self-serving—a calculated effort to save face and guarantee that his legacy would not be tarnished. This stratagem worked well, for this incident has been conveniently overlooked by all Mossman's biographers.[47]

After hearing of Chacón's capture near the Sneed Ranch, and how his remuda of horses had been endangered, Frank B. Mason of the Greene Cattle Company "expressed himself as extremely gratified." This was reported in the *Daily Review* on September 6. The following day, *The Tombstone Epitaph*, being a weekly newspaper published only on Sundays, finally reported the news of Chacón's capture. Its coverage of the event did not deviate much from the version of the story reported initially by the *Bisbee Daily Review*, except that the Tombstone paper implicated Chacón and his gang in the murders of "two prospectors in the fall of 1896 on Eagle creek" and that of "a lone prospector, whom they killed, and then threw his body down an old shaft." Chacón and Alvord's theft of the horses from the Warren Ranch was also noted.

The Mossman Version

Two days after the first report of Chacón's capture appeared in the *Bisbee Daily Review*, a second variation of the story, gleaned primarily from an interview with Mossman himself, was published by the newspaper. This version of the story was a significant departure from the "media version." To begin with, the *Daily Review* found it necessary to recount Chacón's legacy of crime. In this highly fictionalized exposé, it was said that Chacón began his criminal career a decade before as a smuggler in Cochise County, making his headquarters in Bisbee. While residing there, it was said that he was arrested "several times" for petty offenses. This statement is probably hyperbole, as there are no extant records of any arrests or indictments for Chacón.

Then, in 1896 or 1897, Chacón was said to have moved his base of operations to Graham County, "where he stole horses and cattle and escaped into Mexico." The newspaper recounted the tale of the robbery of McCormick's store in Morenci but altered it significantly in order to make it more sensational. Paul Becker was said to have been "almost cut to pieces by the gang of Mexican cut throats" and left lying on the floor inside the store. He was found by the store clerks coming into work the following morning, "almost dead from loss of blood." Additionally, the cash drawer was reported to have been emptied and several hundred dollars in merchandise stolen.

The story of the killing of Pablo Salcido was also embellished by the *Daily Review*. A posse led by Deputy Sheriff Davis, which included Salcido and a man named "Dutch" Keppler, found and followed the blood trail from McCormick's mercantile to "a Mexican cabin." Upon seeing the approaching posse, Chacón and two others bolted from the house and began clambering up the hill. The officers gave chase. A "running fight ensued," during which only one of the suspects was reported to have been killed. Chacón was reportedly wounded, but not before he did for Salcido. Chacón was subsequently taken to Solomonville, tried and, being found guilty of murder, sentenced to hang. In the newspaper's account of Chacón's escape, the sleeping guards were not given mention.

Mossman's story of the capture of Chacón began with the former captain realizing that a raid on Chacón in his stronghold would be futile—"[t]hat plan had been tried time and time again, but met with defeat." Only through "strategy and cunning" would the outlaw be captured. To this end, Mossman recruited Billy Stiles, the Cochise train robber and the man who freed Alvord from the Tombstone jail after shooting the jailor in the leg, and "enlisted him as a member of the ranger company."

Stiles was then sent out "to cultivate the acquaintance of Chacón." By the most fortunate of coincidences, Stiles was renting a house from "a relative of Chacón" in Cananea and managed to get an introduction to the outlaw through this unnamed person. A few weeks later, Stiles sent Chacón a message saying that he knew of a ranch just north of the border where they could, with a minimal amount of effort, liberate some horses. "Several messages were sent back and forth, a meeting was arranged, and the details of the raid in the Sneed pasture near Naco were formulated." According to Mossman, Stiles and Chacón agreed to meet outside the town of Naco early on Wednesday evening.

Stiles brought Mossman to the meeting, introducing the ex-captain as a fellow outlaw, and informing Chacón that Mossman would be accompanying them on the raid. It seems rather unlikely that Chacón would have assented to take along someone he was not acquainted with, but for some reason, he was said to have agreed to this. Stiles then went into Naco to buy some whiskey, leaving Chacón alone with Mossman. When Stiles returned, the three men proceeded to Sneed's Ranch, arriving there at about eleven o'clock. As the night was exceptionally dark, it was decided to wait until morning to proceed with the theft. "The three men dismounted, tied their horses, and, with the bottle of whiskey, proceeded to pass the night away telling stories, in which Chacón took a lively interest."

According to Mossman's account, as dawn approached, the trio built a small fire, over which they cooked their breakfast, which consisted of bacon and coffee, made with "dirty water" Stiles had procured from a nearby pool. As they ate, Chacón began to grow anxious, refusing to indulge in anymore whiskey. He began questioning Mossman. Chacón first admired and commented on the lawman's cartridge belt and pistol. Then the outlaw asked to examine Mossman's rifle. This Mossman said he allowed, while keeping his "six-shooter in easy reach." Slowly, the former Ranger said, it "dawned on the outlaw he had been trapped, although by neither look nor sign did he betray his feelings."

After the three men finished their meager breakfast, Stiles and Chacón sat on the ground and began rolling some cigarettes. Mossman stated that Chacón continued to watch him "like a hawk." As casually as possible, Mossman approached the outlaw and asked him for a cigarette. After receiving one, Mossman returned to the campfire, lit the smoke and then turned and started back toward the seated men. Mossman said, "Well, Bill…" and pulled his revolver, aiming it directly at Chacón. A moment later, Stiles was jabbing Chacón in the ribs with his pistol. "The trick had been done," declared the *Daily Review*.

"Chacón," Mossman said, "never made a move." He only looked into the lawman's eyes and, with "a sinicle [*sic*] smile, said, '*Mátame.¿Por qué no te adelantas y me matas?*' [Kill me. Why don't you go ahead and kill me?]" Mossman did not say what his reply was. Stiles proceeded to relieve Chacón of his gun belt and handcuff him. Mossman, Stiles and Chacón then mounted up and began the journey back to the train station at Naco.

"Hand's Up." Chacón's arrest imagined by F. Golcurn Clark from *Pearson's Magazine* (January 1905). *Author's collection.*

"This was the story of the capture of Chacón as told *The Review* by Captain Mossman."

Again, as with the "media version," there are parts of the tale that do not appear credible, such as Stiles just happening to live in a house owned by one of Chacón's relatives and Chacón putting such trust in Stiles, whom he had only recently met, to agree to go on a raid with the man. Further, there is the issue of the legitimacy and legality of the entire venture. As noted, Mossman had officially resigned his captain's commission on September 1, and yet he stated that he had deputized Stiles as an Arizona Ranger. Was it within Mossman's authority to make this appointment? As will be seen, ex-captain Mossman was not entirely forthcoming with the press during this interview.

In its "City News in Brief" column of September 10, the *Daily Review* revealed that upon his arrival in Naco, Chacón's personal belongings—his cartridge belt, pistol, bowie knife, Winchester, spurs and so on—were appropriated by the locals. Stiles permitted this and possibly even profited from it. "[E]verybody grabbed something as a souvenir of the capture of the noted outlaw." That same day, the *Arizona Sentinel* of Yuma made the allegation that Chacón was actually taken captive in Sonora, and not the United States, as Mossman had claimed, which would have been in violation of international law. This accusation would be repeated again and again.

The most ludicrous of the variation of the story of Chacón's capture was published in the *Arizona Silver Belt* on September 11. The newspaper stated that Stiles and Mossman were identified as deputy U.S. marshals and that the capture of the Chacón was effected at the Greene Ranch near Hereford. The newspaper reported that at about daybreak, Chacón arrived at the ranch with Stiles and "another Mexican." Mossman, and a third, unidentified officer, were hiding "in the brush near the pasture gates." When Chacón dismounted to open the gate, the intrepid Mossman leaped out from his place of concealment and covered Chacón with his weapon, while Stiles drew down on Chacón's friend. The two outlaws were then secured, transported to Packard Station and put aboard a train for Solomonville.

Aside from the numerous inaccuracies and inconsistencies contained in the article, what is notable about the *Silver Belt* account is it is the first to make mention of Burt Alvord's involvement in the capture of Chacón. According the newspaper, Stiles had been introduced to Chacón by Burt Alvord in Sonora, not by a relative, as Mossman had previously asserted. This begs the question: if Alvord had been integral to the capture of Chacón, why had Mossman not acknowledged his involvement?

On this same date, the *Copper Era* acknowledged its earlier error in crediting the capture of Chacón to Sheriff James Parks. Parks had received a telegraph prior to the apprehension of the fugitive and was "en route to that section" when Chacón was taken. "Mr. Parks had been laboring to capture Chacón ever since his introduction into the sheriff's office, and several times he was close on the trail, but the wiley [*sic*] old outlaw always managed to give him the slip." The newspaper was not deriding or censuring Sheriff Parks by any means and ended the column by calling him "one of the best sheriffs in Arizona."[48]

The Alvord Version

The *Tucson Citizen*, which was the first among the territorial newspapers to break the news of Chacón's capture, albeit with several errors, scored another exclusive in reporting the surrender of Burt Alvord to Cochise County sheriff Adelbert Lewis. To the surprise of the citizenry of Tucson, Sheriff Lewis, Billy Stiles and Alvord stepped off the train at the Southern & Pacific Depot at about eleven o'clock on the morning of the eleventh and took what appeared to be a very leisurely stroll down Congress Street, as though they were tourists taking in the sights. Even more remarkable was the fact that Alvord was neither cuffed nor shackled, "and the sheriff did not seem the least fearful about the security of his captive."

The destination of the party was the Pima County Sheriff's Office, and upon their arrival there, the reporter for the *Citizen* was invited to sit in on the conference. He learned that "Alvord was not captured, but surrendered

The town of Tucson, Arizona Territory. *Author's collection.*

himself of his own free will." The outlaw complained that he had grown tired of "his rough and desperate life in Mexico" and had contacted his friend Stiles to say that he would turn himself in if the authorities could promise him "a square deal." Stiles, "anxious to aid his old friend," had gone to Sheriff Lewis with the proposal and had extracted a promise from the Sheriff that Alvord would be shown "all the leniency possible under the circumstances." Stiles returned to Alvord with the news, "and a meeting was arranged."

As previously agreed, Sheriff Lewis, Stiles and Alvord met on the evening of September 10 on the Mexican side of the border, and Alvord turned himself in. Sheriff Lewis and Billy Stiles escorted the former fugitive back across the line, where the three of them boarded a train that delivered them to Tucson the following morning. "The prisoner was brought to the city today to transact some business at this point," reported the *Citizen*. "He was placed in a cell in the county jail. He will be taken back to Tombstone shortly, and will face any charges that may be brought against him at the next term of the court."

Aside from the surprising news of Burt Alvord's surrender, the *Tucson Citizen* provided its readers new revelations about the capture of Augustine Chacón (whom the newspaper continued to refer to as "Juan Chacón"). The newspaper asserted that Alvord, not Mossman and Stiles, was "the real captor of the noted criminal, and the credit is due him for the man being taken as he was." After this declaration, the *Citizen* proceeded to report the details said to have been related to the reporter by Alvord himself.

Alvord stated that he had been "acquainted with Chacón" but stopped short of saying how they had been introduced or by whom. Alvord said it was he who had "induced him to come across the line for the alleged purpose of stealing horses at Sneed's ranch." Alvord and Chacón met Stiles outside of Naco, and it was Stiles who decided that they would wait until daylight before proceeding with the theft. Stiles also told Chacón that one of the men who had escaped from the jail in Tombstone with Alvord and him would be joining them. "Chacón did not like 'gringoes [*sic*],' but readily agreed." The trio met Mossman at the ranch at about eleven o'clock that night.

By the following morning, Chacón had become rather wary "of the Tombstone jail breaker, the guise Mossman assumed, and watched him closely." Alvord stated that he left, as he did not want "to witness the capture." One may wonder if, as Alvord said, his departure was due to pangs of conscience about betraying a friend, or if he worried that Stiles and Mossman might decide to attempt to take both him and Chacón at the same time. "At the appointed moment, Mossman covered his man, and Billy Stiles did the same." Chacón was said to have "sneeringly asked them to shoot him, but it was too late. He had been tricked and was a prisoner."

The reporter for the *Citizen* concluded that "efforts will be made to have Alvord let off light when he is brought to trial."

The Second Mossman Version

The very next day, September 12, the *Bisbee Daily Review* featured another interview with former captain Mossman, which was likely given in response to Alvord's revelations regarding his role in the capture of Chacón. It seems that Mossman was very upset with Billy Stiles, as Stiles was supposed to arrange for Alvord to surrender to him, not to Sheriff Lewis. In this second interview, Mossman again recounted the story of the capture of Chacón, though modifying his original tale to include Alvord. "I was determined, if possible, to capture Chacón," said the former Ranger captain, "and made Stiles one of my rangers to assist me, as he was in with Chacón and Alvord. Stiles told me where Alvord was, and I went to see him."

Mossman stated that on April 21, he had traveled down to Minas Piertas, a small hamlet located "about fifty miles from Guaymas, Mexico." Alvord was holed up in a residence there with "a band of Mexican outlaws," and Mossman said that he made his camp nearby. "I went there alone, and was met at the door by Mexican's [*sic*] rifles. I had never seen Alvord, and he had never seen me, but I stayed at this camp about twenty-four hours." During his stay, Mossman said that he spoke with Alvord, informing him of his intention to capture Chacón, and asked for Alvord's assistance. Alvord, whom Mossman said "was tired of that kind of life," agreed to help, though probably not before extracting promises from Mossman to assist him in his legal plight.

About a month went by before Captain Mossman met with Alvord again, this time in Naco. At this meeting, Alvord said that he had not yet found Chacón "and did not know where he was." Chacón would later state that he was still enlisted as a soldier when Alvord first contacted him. "I asked permission to go out to meet him," said Chacón, "as I knew he was near the place at which I was stationed, and he sent word that he wished to see me, but I was not allowed to go, and he came to see me.…He asked me to travel with him in his company, and my answer to him was that I could not, because I did not wish to return to the United States, and that I did not have horse, saddle or ammunition."

"I heard from [Alvord] a short while later," Mossman told the *Daily Review*, "after he had located Chacón, and he came along with him when I captured him. Chacón, Alvord, and myself were together when Stiles rode into Naco to get some grub and some whiskey, and when we went to camp that night, Alvord left us." This was all Mossman would have to say on this subject of Alvord's involvement in the apprehension of Chacón, but he railed on about Billy Stiles's duplicity. "It was understood that Stiles was to keep me posted as to the time when Alvord was to give himself up." On Wednesday, September 10, Mossman received a telephone message from Stiles and immediately left for Naco to meet him.

"Stiles met me at the livery stable, and told me Alvord was there or would be there. I went across the line to Stiles' house, and then he told me he had been mistreated, and that he had not received the amount of money the rangers had promised. I told him this was a pretty time to say so," recalled Mossman, "and asked him why he did not say so across the line, and some hot words followed." Mossman then left Stiles and went back across the line. According to Mossman, what had upset Stiles was the fact that Thomas Harbo Rynning, who had succeeded Mossman as captain of the Arizona Rangers, "would not have him on the force."

Captain Thomas Harbo Rynning. *Arizona State Library Archives & Public Records, History and Archives Division, Phoenix, #96-2504.*

Stiles purportedly told Mossman that he would meet him back across the line, but he never showed. "[Sheriff] Dell Lewis told me that Stiles came to him later, and asked him if he wanted to see Alvord, and this was the first he knew Alvord was there," insisted Mossman. "[Lewis] went out a short distance from Naco with Stiles, and found Alvord, who gave himself up." Further, Mossman said that he had spoken to Alvord directly and claimed that Alvord stated he had wanted to give himself up to Mossman, "but it was on Stiles' account he did not." On the eighteenth, the *Copper Era* elaborated on the story of Stiles' subterfuge, saying that Stiles had "contracted" to turn Alvord over to Mossman but, after the "misunderstanding" about the payment, changed his mind and contacted Sheriff Lewis.

"Stiles neglected to inform Mossman of his intention in this regard, hence Mossman did not know the surrender was made," reported the Clifton newspaper. "On the day of the surrender, Mossman was riding his horse along the railroad track near Don Luis station, when he met the train bearing Sheriff Louis [*sic*], Billy Stiles, and Alvord. Mossman was so infuriated that he put spurs his horse [*sic*] and for some distance pursued the train, emptying his six-shooter over the rear car." The *Daily Review* made light of this incident, saying that Mossman was in a "hilarious mood" and had been entertained the passengers of the train with "an exhibition of fast shooting and rough riding." It was stated that Conductor Brown and several passengers "expressed themselves in no uncertain tones regarding the actions of Mossman."

As perturbed as former captain Mossman seems to have been about Stiles thwarting his plan to bring in Burt Alvord, one begins to suspect that his motivation was not actually the serving of justice, but something more personal. Doubtlessly, bringing in both Chacón and Alvord would have put a new shine on his tarnished reputation. Perhaps Mossman expected that by bringing in these two celebrated criminals in such a short space of time, he would be redeemed in the eyes of the public for his previous transgressions and possibly even be reinstated as an Arizona Ranger. Alas, this was not to be.

"That Stiles failed to carry out the programme as originally intended was only another exhibition of the peculiarities of this individual," said the *Daily Review*. It added that Sheriff Lewis was "simply performing his duty as a public officer....Whether the train robber [Alvord] surrendered to Sheriff Del Lewis, of Cochise county, or to ex-Captain Burton C. Mossman, of the rangers, is of no importance."[49]

Author Ryder Ridgway, in the second volume of *Mt. Graham Profiles*, included an anecdote that has very rarely, if ever, been told concerning Chacón and Sheriff Parks. Allegedly, upon their return to Solomonville, Chacón told the lawman that he had once had the opportunity to kill him, but had desisted. "I was in that cave at Ash Spring the time you and your wife passed," said the outlaw. Parks later told Ridgway that he recalled the incident. He remembered that it was about dusk when he and his wife were driving though the section, and he observed a man come out of a cave up on the hillside. "I saw the fellow had a gun, so I handed the reins to my wife, and laid my Winchester across my lap. I never realized it was Chacón until he reminded me of the incident."

Unfortunately, there is no way to authenticate this story. However, one can see why this particular tale is rarely retold, as it contradicts the entire Chacón legend. Assuming that Chacón actually was the sociopathic murderer the press made him out to be, why would he not have shot Sheriff Parks when he had the chance? It is clear that Chacón had the drop on him from the time he came out of the cave, and the killing of a county sheriff, even from ambush, would have bolstered his reputation among the outlaw fraternity he allegedly kept company with. Of course, some might argue that Chacón showed mercy because Sheriff Parks was with his wife, but according to the legend, Chacón was not averse to killing women. Why then would Chacón not kill Sheriff Parks when the opportunity presented?

The act—or the lack thereof—certainly does not fit with what has been written about the Chacón, either in contemporary newspapers or by modern authors. It is very much out of character, especially for man who had been charged by the press with killing so many others. Then again, this is all just conjecture—supposition about a story that may not even be true.

Eight days after the event occurred, on September 12, the *Graham Guardian*, a weekly newspaper and, arguably, the one most invested in the story of Augustine Chacón, finally printed its account of his apprehension. One would think that, having had time to peruse the accounts provided by the other territorial newspapers, the *Guardian* would have narrated the story with some accuracy, but it did not. What the newspaper printed was a slight variation on the "Mossman version." What is of significance, and relevant to this study, are the peripheral stories that the newspaper told about Chacón, which may well have served as the rudiment for some of the modern tales about Chacón.

After describing the outlaw as "a bold, desperate man who, it is said, never allowed a human life to stand between him and the accomplishment of his designs," the *Guardian* went on to say, "Chacón has been an outlaw in Arizona for 20 years. He gave Sheriff Slaughter, of Cochise county, no end of trouble. The sheriff and Burt Alvord and other deputies traveled hundreds of miles chasing Chacón and his gang." In an anecdote, which is without any foundation or corroboration from existing historical records, it was stated that one night "a posse of two or three" discovered Chacón and his gang's hideout in the mountains and had attacked it. "In the fight that followed, two of the gang were killed. Chacón made his escape, but carried away a charge of buckshot away with him."

The *Guardian* proceeded to recount the story of the burglary of McCormick's store and the stabbing of Becker. The firefight on the hillside between Officer Davis and Chacón, Luna and Morales was also reiterated, but with Pablo Salcido cast not as the pistol-waving hothead, ignoring Deputy Davis's admonishments, but as a non-threatening mediator, attempting to talk to the suspects and induce them to surrender peacefully. Upon seeing Salcido approaching on his placatory mission, "one of the Mexicans, supposed to be Chacón, raised up, rested the rifle across the boulder, took deliberate aim, fired" and killed the ineffectual Morenci saloonkeeper in cold blood.

Chacón's indictment, trial, conviction and sentencing by Justice Rouse were all mentioned briefly, as was his appeal. His escape was described in some detail, but again, there was no acknowledgement of the two slumbering guards. Since his jail delivery, "Sheriffs Birchfield, Clark, and Parks have all made determined efforts to capture the outlaw," but without success. Sheriff Parks, the newspaper said, had come closest to nabbing Chacón, when the outlaw "attempted to go to Morenci, but the sherfff [*sic*] was after him so quick that he got back into Mexico on a hot trail."

The *Guardian* went on to accuse Chacón of "at least four murders," said to have been committed since his escape from the Solomonville jail. "It is said that a strong effort will now be made to get his sentence commuted to life imprisonment, but this will hardly succeed for, if he was guilty of murdering Pabalo [*sic*] Salcido in 1895, he is equally guilty now." Public opinion, which was predominantly dictated by the newspapers, had already sealed the fate of Augustine Chacón. The rest would be simply a matter of formality.[50]

As the Fates Decreed

Albert W. "Burt" Alvord was acquitted of the territorial charges against him, mostly in light of his having been instrumental in the capture of Chacón, However, the federal court was unimpressed by his betrayal of his friend, and Alvord was indicted for "Interfering with the U.S. Mails." On December 8, Alvord pleaded guilty to the charge and was sentenced to two years in the Arizona Territorial Penitentiary. After thinking on it, Alvord decided that he did not want to do the time, and on December 15, 1903, he and Billy Stiles, who had also been arrested on federal charges, escaped a second time from the Cochise County Jail in Tombstone. This time around, Alvord's freedom was short-lived. He was recaptured after being wounded in a firefight with Sheriff Lewis and a posse of officers at the Young Ranch, outside of Naco, on February 17, 1904.

After his leg wound was treated, Alvord was transported to the Territorial Penitentiary in Yuma to serve out his two-year sentence. Upon his release, on October 9, 1906, Alvord relocated to California, where he had a sister living. However, there were still unresolved indictments against him, and warrants had been issued by the territorial authorities. Before these warrants could be served, Alvord absconded to South America, never to return to the United States. The information available about his remaining years in that region of the world largely comprises speculation and conjecture. On July 29, 1910, the *Graham Guardian* announced that Albert Wright "Burt" Alvord had died of fever at Barbados [*sic*] in the West Indies three months prior.[51]

Billy Stiles was with Burt Alvord at the Young Ranch in Naco when Sheriff Lewis and his posse laid siege to that place and shot Alvord through the leg. Stiles, whose sense of self-preservation seems to have been much more developed than that of any of his confederates, skinned out and left Alvord to his fate. Having saved his own hide once again, Billy Stiles did what so many other outlaws had tried to do before him but had failed at: he disappeared. Rumors about his whereabouts and purported sightings continued to appear in the territorial newspapers for years afterward, especially after Alvord was released from prison. The two were reported to be seen together several times, just as they had been in "the old days."

When Stiles finally resurfaced in December 1908, the circumstances were so incredible that it was treated by most the newspapers with the utmost skepticism. On Saturday, December 5, Stiles, who had assumed the name "William Larkin" in his capacity as a deputy sheriff of Humbolt County, Nevada, was attempting to serve some papers in civil suit when he was shot to death by Charles Barr at King's River Ranch, about ninety miles from the town of Winnemucca. In what some might view as a case of poetic justice, Barr shot Stiles in the back three times. A few years later, Charles Barr was arrested for robbing a streetcar in Pueblo, Colorado, and then tried, found guilty and imprisoned for a term of twelve to sixteen years. But he was never held to answer for the killing of Stiles (aka Deputy Sheriff Larkin).

Even after Stiles's long-suffering wife, Maria, wrote a letter to the *Bisbee Daily Review* stating emphatically that her husband was dead, some persons refused to believe Billy Stiles had been killed and even came up with an elaborate theory in which Stiles's sister-in-law, Luisa, in collusion with Maria, had perpetuated a masterful hoax, substituting the body of another for that of Stiles, so Stiles could finally disappear for good. The tales told concerning Stiles, replete with contrived evidence seeming to indicate that he might well still be alive, somehow and somewhere, made for good copy, but in the end, they were probably just that—tales.

Most ironically, in a twist that Stiles might well have found amusing, the name of Deputy Sheriff William Larkin "Billy" Stiles can be found listed on several modern internet sites dedicated to law enforcement officers killed in the line of duty, including the American Peace Officer Virtual Museum and the James D. Hoff Peace Officer Memorial.[52]

Burt Mossman never worked in law enforcement again, although he regularly regaled gullible reporters with tales of his glory days as the captain of the Arizona Rangers and the capture of Augustine Chacón. Mossman, who had been co-owner of the Tovrea & Mossman, Wholesale and Retail Butchers in Bisbee, sold his interest in that business and moved to Seattle, Washington, in November 1902. By the following year, Mossman was employed as the superintendent of the Hanford Cattle Company in McMillen, New Mexico. In December 1905, he married Miss Grace Eleanor Coburn of Kansas City, the daughter of one of his business partners. The *Arizona Republican* stated that he "divided his time between McMillen and South Dakota, where he has a big cattle ranch of his own on the Sioux Indian Reservation."

To accommodate their booming business, Mossman and his partners—including Colonel William C. Greene, who owned the Sneed Ranch, where Chacón was caught—acquired more acreage in New Mexico, near the town of Roswell. Mossman continued on in the cattle business for several decades, with great success, and the Arizona newspapers routinely made mention of the former captain whenever he visited the territory/state. Inevitably, in these reports, Mossman, who retained the honorific title of "Captain," would be lauded as the captor of the infamous outlaw Augustine Chacón. The apprehension of Chacón, as underhanded as it was, had become the shining moment of his brief career in law enforcement.

Captain Burton Charles "Burt" Mossman died in Roswell, New Mexico, on September 5, 1956, at the age of eighty-nine, leaving behind his second wife, Ruth Schrader of Texas; a son, Burton Charles Jr.; and a daughter, Mary C. His first wife, Grace, had died in 1909, soon after the birth of their daughter, and he remarried in 1925. He was interred at the Mount

Washington Cemetery in Independence, Missouri. In 1960, Captain Mossman was inducted into the Hall of Great Westerners, one of three halls of fame administered by the National Cowboy & Western Heritage Museum in Oklahoma City.[53]

CHAPTER 7

A LEGAL LYNCHING

In an opinion piece titled "Outlawry in Arizona," the managing editor of the *Bisbee Daily Review*, William Kelly, very neatly summarized the inherent anxieties and attendant racism of the majority of Anglo population of his era:

> *Along the border there is and always will be desperadoes of all classes, who are fugitives from justice, and, like wild animals, must live on what chance prey comes to their hands, living far from civilization and in the most inaccessible fastness. There is another class along the border, better only in a degree. Outwardly, they are law-abiding citizens, but secretly, either by common sympathy or through fear of their vengeance, shield and protect them from their deserts. No criminal is too low to have his friends, staunch and true, to whom he can entrust his life and liberty.*
>
> *It is only occasionally that one of these ruffians, by fortuitous circumstances, or by superior skill in crime, makes such a record that it stands out prominently on the dark and bloody background of border crime. The longer such an* [sic] *one goes free, the more dangerous he becomes to the community, for gradually he draws to him the most desperate of his fellows and they levy tribute with impunity. Opposition to their will is certain death.*
>
> *Romance steps in and with her mystic fingers wreathes tales that fascinate the imagination. The bandit becomes a hero and his simplest actions are magnified into glorious deeds. His bloodiest work is taken as a*

> *matter of course and judged by a standard all its own, which eliminates the brutal and magnifies the daring.*
>
> *In a degree, Chacón, recently caught at Naco, is such a man. Not so much among Americans is this true, as among the Mexicans, to whom his deeds have become a subject for twilight tales—a bugaboo to frighten children into obedience.*
>
> *It will be well indeed for law and order if Chacón and those of his class get the penalties prescribed by law for their crimes. Close contact dispels the golden mists of romance and the prisoner appears in his cell, little better than a wild animal in its cage, ever alert for an opportunity to escape and do more violence—so sunk in degradation as to cherish but one idea—revenge.*

Of course, when the editor spoke about the "classes along the border," he was speaking primarily of the Hispanic population. Kelly as much as said this when he posited that it was "the Mexicans," and "not so much" the Americans, who elevated outlaws to the status of heroes. This, and the fact it was Chacón—a renowned Mexican bandit—about whom the editor was writing. The entire article was a thinly veiled denunciation of the Hispanic population in which Kelly reeled off a number of racist attributes that Anglos regularly imbued persons of Hispanic heritage with—an animalistic nature, moral degeneracy, degradation, duplicity and a predilection toward violence.

Kelly gave voice to the xenophobia common to the Anglo population, declaring that Hispanics of the region were either all-out criminals or, even if they appeared to be law-abiding, were secretly in sympathy with the criminals. His message was clear: none of the Hispanics could be trusted. When Kelly stated that the ascendant bandit was a danger to the community, it was implicitly understood that he was speaking of the Anglo-American community. It is almost amusing when Kelly asserts that Chacón has been made into "a bugaboo to frighten children into obedience." In fact, the territorial press had long before made Chacón "a bugaboo" to frighten the Anglos—a malevolent and malicious Mexican monster hiding among and/or being hidden by the Hispanic population. As a rapacious and relentless criminal legend, galloping to and fro across the borderlands, Chacón had become the very embodiment of the threat that Anglo-Americans believed the Hispanic population posed to their culture and civilization.

Chacón's execution was a reaction to this perceived threat. It was, for all intents and purposes, a legal lynching. It was a demonstration of the absolutist cultural hegemony of the Anglo or "white race" and a reminder to the Hispanic population of their proper place as second-class citizens within this Anglo-American hierarchical construct. The message being sent to these persons of Hispanic heritage was clear: Those who acquiesced and submitted to the dominion of the established order and the ascendant authority of the Anglos would be relatively safe in person and property, but those like Chacón, who sought to undermine or subvert the established order, would be dealt with most harshly.

The execution of Chacón was proclaimed as necessary and just by the territorial press. "The only power that can save Chacón," stated the *Bisbee Daily Review* of October 7, "is the Governor of Arizona, or the President of the United States. Chacón will hang and serve as an example to others of his class." As argued earlier, the word *class* was nothing more than a euphemism for "race."[54]

Nationally, the press had a field day with the capture of Chacón and the subsequent surrender of Alvord. To compile a comprehensive list all of newspapers that carried the news of these two events would be a monumental chore and, quite frankly, a tedious read. Suffice it to say, the news was disseminated from one coast to the other. What becomes apparent as one peruses some of these press announcements is how differently Chacón and Alvord were characterized in the press. Descriptors such as "desperate," "notorious," "bloodthirsty" and "murderous" were commonly employed in the description of "the noted Mexican bandit."

The *Los Angeles Times* called Chacón "one of the most lurid dime-novel bandits the Southwest has ever known," while the *Boston Post* said, "Chacón is a good-looking Mexican when in jail and smooth-shaven, but when at large he wears a heavy beard, which gives him a sinister appearance, and gained him the nickname '*El Peludo*,' which is the Mexican word for the long-haired man." The *Post* also accused him of slaying twenty-three men, "either from ambush or killed in open fight."

By sharp contrast, Burt Alvord was portrayed as a tragic and damaged human being, almost to be sympathized with. The *San Francisco Chronicle* described him thus: "Hunted by rangers in the United States and the *rurales* in Mexico, his right arm shattered by bullets so that he could no longer use a gun, with a bullet lodged in his left leg, Alvord became cast down, lost his iron nerve, and made up his mind to surrender on the best possible terms." Said the *Los Angeles Times* of Alvord, "The desperado seems broken in spirit. The novelty of the life has worn off, and the palmy days of twenty years ago are no more."

Associate Justice Fletcher Morris Dunn. *Arizona Historical Society, PC 1000, Main Photo Collection, Portraits—Doan, Mr. & Mrs. Fletcher Morris (Anne Murray), #72094.*

Notable is the *Boston Post*'s use of the moniker "*El Peludo*" as a nickname for Chacón. This appears to be the first time this sobriquet, correctly spelled and translated, was utilized by the press.

This same article would be reprinted in several other national newspapers, including the *Butte Miner* and the *Baltimore Sun*. The long-awaited apprehension of Chacón was big news, worthy of full-page exposé in the *San Francisco Examiner*, replete with an attention-grabbing headline—"King of the Arizona Desperadoes"—and lurid illustrations depicting Chacón in profile, his jailbreak and his capture.[55]

To no one's surprise, Associate Justice Fletcher M. Doan had, on October 9, 1902, after a brief review of the case, upheld the sentence originally imposed by Justice Rouse in 1896, despite the fact that Rouse had said he would not have sentenced Chacón to hang if he had any legal alternative. However, by this juncture, with all that had been written about Chacón in the newspapers, territorial and national—the many tales of his murderous appetites and the numerous killings erroneously attributed to him—it had gone too far, and the allegations could not be retracted or the course reversed. The lies of the newspapers had become truths to the public, and the public's demand for "justice" could and would not be tempered.

Attorney Joseph "Joe" Campbell, who was appointed to represent Chacón at his hearing, "argued at great length and presented many authorities in asking that the prisoner be discharged, because, in the month of March, 1897, the Arizona Territorial Legislature repealed the law of murder without any saving clause to meet the cases where criminals had been indicted under the old law." As discussed previously, this oversight by the legislature should have had the effect of annulling Chacón's conviction or, at the very least, made it only possible for the court to sentence him to ten years for manslaughter. "Judge Doan held that the supreme court had already passed on that question."

No one was going to stand up for Chacón. To have challenged the common assumption that Chacón was guilty, and mitigate his sentence, would be to expose the territorial justice system as fundamentally flawed, to indict the press corps as audacious liars, and to impugn the general public as being the (willing) dupes of these yellow journalists. This would have amounted to political and social suicide for Justice Doan or any other person who attempted it. The court of popular opinion, prejudiced by the media, had declared Chacón to be guilty. It was "common knowledge" that he had committed numerous crimes and, therefore, was deserving of the punishment that awaited him. The legal apparatus was not simply hanging a man. Chacón had long since been elevated above such mundane a station. It was hanging an icon, a veritable legend, one that it had, in collusion with territorial press, created.

The *Bisbee Daily Review* reported, "The mere suggestion that there was a possibility of Chacón's release," however unlikely, "brought a large crowd to the court house, and the court room was packed during the argument of counsel." More likely, the crowd was drawn by the chance to see the legendary Chacón and see what the notorious man-slayer looked like. One wonders if the public was disappointed to find a rather average-looking man sitting in the defendant's chair, "looking pale from his close confinement," his face "covered with a stubby growth of beard" and not at all like the bloodthirsty monster in the press's depiction.

Upon making his ruling, Justice Doan set Chacón's execution for November 21, 1902. Attorney Campbell immediately filed a notice of appeal. The *Daily Review* stated, "The Chacón case may again reach the supreme court," which would have the effect of giving Chacón another year's lease on life. The *Copper Era* added, "The prisoner's release [was] asked for on Habeas Corpus proceedings." The prosecutors, Wiley E. Jones and Thomas S. Bunch, "both special counsels for the territory," stated that they would resist the appeal and predicted that the execution would go on as scheduled, "unless the governor of the territory should come to his relief."

On November 7, the *Arizona Republican* published its report on the case of Augustine Chacón. The newspaper stated that his conviction for the murder had been duly upheld, "and the day of execution set for Nov. 21." It was further stated that the hanging would be conducted in the courtyard of the courthouse in Solomonville, the county seat of Graham. The newspaper went on to speak about the killing of Pablo Salcido, Chacón's trial and conviction and his escape from the county jail. The *Republican* was fairly accurate in its reporting of these events, aside from saying that Salcido had been killed on Christmas Day.

However, the newspaper charged that Chacón had committed eight more murders since his escape but neglected to provide any details that would make this statement believable. "His will not be the first death penalty that has been executed in Graham county," noted the journalist. "As early as '82, three Indian police, who turned traitors against the government, were hanged at [Fort] Grant. Several Mexicans have also been hanged; the last execution occurring only a few years ago." The newspaper reported that special invitations had been distributed by the sheriff's office "to a select few to witness a hardened soul launched into eternity." In closing, the reporter became philosophical, asking, "Don't men need a spectacle of something more elevating than [a hanging]?"

The overall tone of the article, the strict adherence to the facts, without too much hyperbole, and, most particularly, that it really did not provide any new information, strikes one as being a bit contrived. It was almost as though the reporter was attempting to justify the execution of this "hardened soul" for the reader. The two fabrications that were included—that Salcido was killed on Christmas Day and that Chacón had killed eight more people—served only to bolster his argument that Chacón was deserving of the noose. When the journalist spoke to the other executions, attempting to make it seem like the hanging of Chacón would be nothing out of the ordinary, one really begins to see his argument for what it really was: a rationalization for a lynching.[56]

Meanwhile, back in Graham County, preparations were being made for the hanging of Augustine Chacón. On the thirteenth, the *Copper Era* reported that Sheriff Parks had issued invitations to the hanging of "Augustus [*sic*] Chacón." The newspaper noted that this would be the lawman's first time conducting an execution but predicted "everything will pass off fine." In fact, Sheriff James Parks was not relishing the thought of having to pull the lever on Chacón. According to Graham County historian Ryder Ridgway, who had the opportunity to speak firsthand with the men involved, the sheriff said, "I didn't want to spring the trap, so I asked John [Epley, the deputy sheriff] if he wanted to do it."

Deputy Epley replied, "Nothing doing. If he tried to get away, I would damn sure shoot him, but I don't want to spring no trap."

Parks's sister, Jennie Parks Ringgold, in her rather contrived memoir, asserted that Sheriff Parks also offered a man named Red Kinsey fifty dollars to "spring the trap." When Kinsey declined, the sheriff reportedly said, "Well, I guess it is my job anyway." Unfortunately, Mrs. Ringgold did not explain why her brother was so reluctant to be the one to actually kill Chacón.

The *Bisbee Daily Review* reported that "Sheriff Parks is making all the necessary arrangements to carry out the death sentence now resting on the noted criminal and outlaw. Guards are doubled at the jail to prevent any possibility of escape by the condemned man." A letter, allegedly written by Chacón, was discovered in the possession of Librado Macias, who was also in jail, awaiting trial for setting fire to bales of hay in San Jose. The letter was addressed to Macias and, on the reverse, had been replied to. It was believed that two female inmates, who were awaiting transfer to the prison at Yuma, had been responsible for passing the letter between the two men. The letter read:

> *Tell me, Macias, why you have been neglecting me so much. Tell me all the news you brought from the outside. That's all.*
>
> *Your sure servant and friend,*
> *AUGUSTIN* [sic] *CHACÓN*

On the other side of the page, Macias had replied:

> *Augustin—I have everything fixed here. They took me because I was drunk last night and they blame me of having set fire to the hay stack. I haven't anything new. I was going to start today for Nogales, but my trip has been stopped. Fafael Martinez was taken in Sonoita. I am your friend as ever.*
>
> *Your friend and sure servant,*
> *LIBRADO MACIAS*

The line from Macias about having "everything fixed" was enough to rattle the county officers, "and the result will be greater vigilance in guarding from now until the day set for hanging Chacón." the *Daily Review* then proceeded to recount in some detail Chacón's crimes and his capture by Mossman, Stiles and Alvord. The report was fairly accurate, except that again it was stated Salcido was killed on Christmas Day while he "was going up the mountain side to persuade Chacón to surrender." The author of the article most conveniently neglected to mention that Salcido was planning to "persuade" Chacón to surrender at the point of a pistol.

To believe that such a letter was actually written, and to believe that the contents of said letter were what was transcribed in the *Daily Review*, one would have to believe that both Chacón and Macias could read and write. Further, the two prisoners would have to be able to read and write English, unless they somehow managed to employ a translator, in addition to finding willingly couriers for the missive. As historian Mary Kay Vaughn asserted, literacy was uncommon among the population of Mexico during this era. Even by 1910, of the estimated 25.1 million persons residing in Mexico, only about 3.3 million could write or read. It is highly unlikely that Chacón was a lettered man. No extant examples of anything he wrote have yet been discovered—not even his signature. This is not to say that this correspondence did not occur, only that is improbable. Since the letter, if there ever was one, has long since disappeared, it is impossible to prove conclusively either way.[57]

The day before Chacón was to be executed, the *Tucson Citizen*, which had finally desisted in calling him "Juan Chacón," instead referring to him as "Gus Chacón," made it known that an application for the writ of habeas corpus had been filed with Associate Supreme Court justice George Russell Davis by Judge William M. Lovell and attorney McCollum. Lowell and McCollum argued that "the murder statute of the Territory, under which Chacón was tried and convicted was repealed March 16, 1897, but after the judgment of death had been pronounced in his case, and it was urged in behalf of the issuance of writ, that his repeal affected the power of the court to make the recent order fixing another date when the former judgment should be executed."

Justice Davis, who was not about to stick his neck out for Chacón and risk the censure of the public, countered, stating that the trial and conviction of Chacón had been completed before the statute was changed and "that sufficient power was given to the court under another continuously existing provision of the law to order the carrying into effect of the original judgment, the validity of which was beyond question." This said, Justice Davis summarily denied the writ. The only thing that was now going to save Chacón would be executive clemency, coming from either the governor, Alexander Bodie, or the president of the country, Theodore Roosevelt.

As far-fetched as a pardon from President Roosevelt might sound, it was actually a very real possibility. As reported in both The *Bisbee Daily Review* and the *Graham Guardian*, *Señor* Manuel Mascareñas, the Mexican consul at Nogales, at the behest of "some men high in authority in Mexico, who are exerting their influence to save the life of the condemned man," visited Chacón on the afternoon of November 17 to interview him in connection with a "hurried investigation" into the death of Pablo Salcido. Mascareñas visited the prisoner twice more that evening. After collecting all the information he could, *Señor* Mascareñas telegraphed his findings to the Mexican ambassador in Washington, D.C.

President Theodore Roosevelt. *Library of Congress.*

"Senor Mascarenas," reported the *Daily Review*, "says it is not the desire of the Mexican government to shield Chacón from punishment, but it would like very much to secure a commutation of sentence to life imprisonment," possibly in light of the fact Chacón had served as a soldier in the Mexican army and had been honorably discharged.

Mascareñas received a reply to his telegram to the Mexican ambassador in Washington, D.C., on Tuesday evening, November 18. The communication

U.S. Secretary of State John Hay. *Library of Congress.*

stated that the ambassador had contacted Secretary of State John Hay and presented his request for the commutation of Chacón's sentence to him, which would then be forwarded to President Roosevelt. It was a long shot, as Roosevelt, like most his contemporaries, was a prejudiced man and was once quoted as saying, "[O]ne of the gravest problems before our people [is]...dealing with the man of color....To solve this problem, it is, of course, necessary to educate him to perform duties, a failure to perform which will render him a curse to himself and to all around him."

The endeavors of *Señor* Mascareñas on Chacón's behalf would come to naught. The *Oasis* reported on November 29, "Friends of Chacón in Mexico had prevailed upon the Mexican government to ask for commutation of sentence to life imprisonment; but action was taken too late to meet all the necessary steps, and the execution proceeded."[58]

On the morning of his execution, Friday, November 21, 1902, Augustine Chacón asked for both breakfast and dinner, which were served to him, and the condemned man "ate heartily of both meals." Chacón then requested a shave and haircut, which Sheriff Parks arranged. He subsequently asked that the local Catholic priest, Father Dertchemont, be summoned. While they awaited the arrival of the priest, Chacón dressed himself in the new black suit that Sheriff Parks had purchased for him. "Chacón requested that he be permitted to speak for one hour from the scaffold, and asked that the sheriff to have Rejino Chavarria, who owns a saloon in Solomonville, [be] present to hear what he would say from the scaffold." Chavarria, it will be remembered, was the man who had testified against Chacón as his trial.

The reporter for the *Graham Guardian* said that Chacón spoke with the priest "several times during the morning," and "seemed to get a great deal of satisfaction from these visits." Just minutes before he was to be walked out to the courtyard, Chacón requested Father Dertchemont return once more. The priest was allowed to enter the cell, and the priest and the prisoner spoke for about five minutes. At about noon, the death march began. Chacón was led from the cell by the officers. He was neither shackled nor cuffed, but rather allowed to go on his own recognizance. As the party exited the building, Sheriff Parks took the lead, followed by Chacón, who was flanked by Deputies Lee Hobbs and John Parks. Father Dertchemont brought up the rear.

About one hundred people were crowded into the small courtyard. "When the scaffold was reached, Chacón mounted it with as much concern as though he were going to a festival." When he had reached the wooden platform at the top of the stairs, Chacón turned to the onlookers and began his statement, speaking entirely in Spanish. His oration was transcribed by stenographer Albert Sames and subsequently translated by Nick Van Alystine:

> *The Statement of Augustin Chacón on the scaffold in the jail enclosure, at Solomonville at 12:50 p.m. November 21st, 1902.*
>
> *I have much to say (asks for a cup of coffee) I desire to speak to all classes of people. I only have three enemies in the country. The names of those three enemies are: one Regino Chaveria* [sic], *the other is Dr.* [William J.] *Davis, and the other is a Mexican, which I have forgotten his name. He lives at Morenci with a woman by the name of Zenovia. It is these three men who have caused my death. Not because I am guilty of what they accuse me of. My conscience is clean. They have tried to give it to me and they have succeeded in doing so. They used the law to bring me up to the scaffold where I am going now to hang. I do not have anything to say*

against the law. God would help us if there was no law, for that reason I say to all of you to be careful and take warning, and have nothing to be guilty of and not have to suffer. I have nothing to say against the relatives of Mr. Pablo—Mr. Pablo Salcido. I do not even have anything against his wife, Louisa. I do not want any of you to believe that I am guilty of the crime. I would not have it done for any thing [sic]. *There are many people here who would pretend to know what they are talking about, but they do not know.*

In regard to my escape from the Solomonville jail five years ago, I want to say that Joe Reaves and George Burkner [the jailors] *are entirely innocent. They would not let me say or do anything that was not so. I wish that God will punish me if I am telling a lie. If I am guilty, I wish to be expelled from His presence like Eve was from Paradise. I carry my conscience clean and bright. I did not do it, but I expect to pay for this crime, because a good many people are in the habit of saying a good many things that are not true, as Mr. Chavaria* [sic] *did. He is the one who ought to be hanged in my stead and for that which I am going to be hanged for to-day. That man did not known* [sic] *because he did not see the killing of Salcido. Nobody can be more satisfied of this than I am myself. I have a clean conscience. I am sure that this hand (raising his right hand) has never been guilty of murder. I may have stolen and done a good many other things, but I am innocent of this crime, from my own knowledge. I want you all to know that my conscience is clean, and never believe that I have been guilty of this crime.*

I have nothing to say against Mr. Wiley Jones, nor nothing to say against Jim Parks or any other official. All that I wish you to think is that I never committed this crime. If all of you are not satisfied and believe I am guilty, I wish that you would tell it to me. (Asks for cigarette papers and rolls cigarette and smokes.)

It is nothing but right that when one is going to die that one be given a few moments of time to quietly smoke a cigarette.

I have been told by several people that I have been in this country since I got away from here. I was here four years ago myself with another party. This party is now dead. I was here for the purpose of knowing how my business was getting on and to hear what was being said about me. That is when I came here I did not come here to do any wrong or harm anybody. I have been told that I have been here since, at different places and different times, with a band of twenty men, and that I have been seen here and there with a band of twenty men. This is not so. At the time I heard this report I was a long distance from here.

I was brought here by a party who told me a lie. This man went to Nacosari [Sonora], *and asked me to come from there. From there we came to near the line, within nine miles. There I was delivered to the Chief of Arizona Rangers. I have been told since that the man who gave me up is in jail at Tombstone. He is said to be in jail and will be dealt with according to law. I could say a good many things against that party, but I will not do so. God will deal with him. I do not wish to see anybody in trouble on my account. I would rather see them out from their troubles than in jail. I wish that God will give him his liberty so that he may not suffer as I have suffered myself. If I am going to suffer death on his account, I wish God to forgive him. I have done lots of favors to get him away from the officers of this country.*

I went to the Yaqui river and enlisted as a soldier at the time the soldiers (Mexican) were there. I was there as a soldier, and the soldiers' quarters are mostas [sic] *bad as it was in jail. I asked permission to go out to meet him as I knew he was near the place at which I was stationed and he sent word that he wished to see me, but I was not allowed to go and he came to see me. I asked him what he was doing, and he told me what he had done and that he was trying to hide away from the officers of the United States. I did not believe his statement. He asked me to travel with him in his company, and my answer to him was that I could not because I did not wish to return to the United States, and that I did not have horse, saddle or ammunition. He then told me that he would provide all these things for me. Fortunately, that day I was discharged—honorably discharged from the army. Then I had to make a night ride for the reason that I wished to get away from him. After that, in September, he was with me again. He told me to come with him that he was going out on an adventure, to look at some mules.*

I told him I would not go with him because the mules were not his, but that they were stolen, and that I did not wish to be in a bad fix with my own country as I was here in the United States. We left that place and the mules were delivered to him by the owner, or rather the one who claimed to be the owner. When we left that day it was raining. Next day about this time we were overtaken by the legitimate owner of the mules. Then he asked me what shall we do, and my answer was that we were in a bad fix. I told him we would try to scare them off by firing on them, but not try to hit any of them, and that would give us a chance to get away. As these mules were stolen, we left them there.

That is the way I have been guilty here and everywhere. It is said that this man (a local Mexican in the audience) a friend of mine has assisted me

> *in different ways in my adventures. It was done in this way that whenever I came to his ranch and asked him for any little favors he complied with my requests as gladly as he would have done with anybody else.*
>
> *I would like if there is anyone around here who has anything against me to come out and say it. Is there is anyone here who has any thing* [sic] *to say against this man? I do not think there is anybody in Clifton or Morenci who can say that I have wronged them. My family is entirely different from what I am, and never was accused of any crime whatever. If I have ever done anything wrong it was here in this country, and I think that all reports about my friend is nothing but a lie.*
>
> *I would like to have you all take care of yourselves and take warning from my case, and not do wrong for if you do you will be dealt with according to law.*
>
> *According to my understanding and knowledge the law is dealt out slowly but surely, with dumb instruments. The law never lets up and never gets out of order. If any of you intend to leave, I would like to have you all remain until the last moment, and now I would like to smoke a cigarette slowly.*

Augustine Chacón then sat down on the scaffold, rolled a second cigarette, lit it and slowly inhaled the smoke. Van Alystine asked if he had any more he wanted to say or if he was finished, to which Chacón replied, "*Sí, es todo.*"

After he finished his cigarette, the condemned man stood back up. He asked that Sisto Molino and Jesus Bustos take charge of his remains after he was dead, and the sheriff agreed to this. "The only evidence of nervousness exhibit [*sic*] was on the scaffold when his eye rested for a moment on the rough casket prepared for his body." Several people stepped forward to shake hands with him one final time. Chacón then asked Sheriff Parks if they could delay until three o'clock. Sheriff Parks said no. Chacón turned to the next person in line to shake his hand and said to him, "It's too late now. Time to hang." He then thanked his jailers.

In the judicial hanging, as this type of execution is commonly referred to, in order to differentiate it from a lynching, the condemned has a noose, typically made of rope, looped once about his neck, and he is dropped through a trapdoor that opens directly beneath his feet. The person is dropped between four and ten feet. At the end of this drop, the noose, if properly positioned, will roll up beneath the jawbone and tighten dramatically, snapping the person's head backward and sideways simultaneously. Ideally, this sudden jerking of the head, referred to as "hyperflexion of the neck," will cause a

Augustine Chacón on the gallows, Solomonville, Arizona Territory. *Arizona Historical Society, PC 161, Ringgold Photo Collection, Box 1, Folder 5, #K.*

dislocation between the C2 and C3 vertebrae. This is commonly known as "a hangman's fracture."

The separation of the vertebra at this point causes either severing or crushing of the spinal cord, resulting in almost instantaneous unconsciousness. In addition, the constriction of the rope about the person's throat will sever or crush the Phrenic nerve, which regulates the diagram, which has the

Augustine Chacón on the gallows, Solomonville, Arizona Territory (second in series). *Arizona Historical Society, PC 161, Ringgold Photo Collection, Box 1, Folder 5, #J.*

effect of discontinuing the person's ability to breathe, and they begin to asphyxiate. The tightening of the rope may also crush the trachea, or "wind pipe," and sever the carotid artery and jugular vein, stopping blood flow to and from the brain, resulting in massive internal bleeding. Fractures of the wings of the hyoid bone and larynx are also common.

As noted, unconsciousness usually occurs within one to three seconds after the drop is completed. However, death is not instantaneous. It may take anywhere from eight to twenty-five minutes for the heart to cease beating.

Brain death, resulting from lack of oxygenated blood being pumped to that organ, is thought to happen more quickly, usually within about six minutes, but this has never been verified by medical science. The limbs may be seen to twitch and move, probably due to involuntary muscle contractions. Also, it is common for sphincter muscles throughout the body to loosen, and the person may urinate and/or defecate. The medical parlance for cause of death in a judicial hanging is "comatose asphyxia."

Chacón asked that the black hood be dispensed with and that his face be left uncovered. Sheriff Parks refused this as well. Chacón removed his own shoes and stood motionless as the lawmen secured the straps around his torso, arms and legs. As Sheriff Parks was pulling the black hood down over his face, Chacón was heard to say, "*Adiós todos mis amigos*." He stood there motionless. At 1:00 p.m., Sheriff Parks sprang the trap, and Chacón plummeted downward. Although his neck was broken immediately, the attending physicians, Drs. Platt and Warner, did not pronounce him dead until twelve minutes after the hour. His remains were then cut down and placed in the pine box by Molino and Bustos, and his corpse was removed to the Catholic church in San Jose.[59]

In her memoir, Ms. Jennie Parks Ringgold, the sister of Sheriff James Parks, asserted that Molino, whom she alleged was a relation to Chacón, conveyed Chacón's corpse via "a wagon and a fast team" to the Catholic church in San Jose, where a priest was waiting. "All that day and night," wrote Ringgold, "the Mexicans worked over the body, rubbing him with alcohol, trying to pour whiskey down his throat, and praying" in an effort to revive the hanged man. "When the efforts proved unavailing, the mortal remains of Chacón were taken out of the church, and buried in the little Catholic cemetery in San Jose."

In fact, as Ryder Ridgway related, Chacón's body was taken to the church not for the purpose of bringing him back from death, but for *el velorio*, or the traditional Mexican wake. "Bustos and Molino…would often chuckle about the many false stories and legends that enveloped their friend, *Peludo*. Both men flatly denied attempting to resuscitate him." Mrs. Catherina Molino was in the church that night, and when she was asked whether Chacón had truly died on the gallows, she replied, "I turned back the sheet and looked at him. He was dead alright. My friend Anita Buttereas stayed all night with me. None of us went to bed."

As was tradition in the Hispanic communities, votive candles were burned and prayers offered up for the soul of the deceased. The body of Chacón was probably washed—a ritual cleansing—and then dressed

Right: Ms. Jennie Parks Ringgold, memoirist. *Graham County Historical Society.*

Below: The San Jose Cemetery in San Jose, Arizona. *Author's photo.*

The grave of Augustine Chacón in San Jose, Arizona. *Author's photo.*

again in preparation for burial. There would have been food served and remembrances and stories about the deceased told by the mourners who gathered there. *El velorio* would have ended with the saying of the Catholic mass for the dead, just prior to the body being transported to the grave site. Ms. Ringgold's absurd story is just that—absurd—and only speaks to her racial prejudice and her deep cultural ignorance.

The body of Augustine Chacón was buried in an unmarked grave at the San Jose Cemetery about three miles from Solomonville. Mrs. Molino recalled that the burial was attended by very few mourners. "Not many of us were there, Jesus Bustos, Jesus Aros, myself, and a few others." Years later, the family (Chacón is believed to have fathered at least one child during his lifetime, although this researcher was unable to find a family history) erected a simple marker that reads, "Augustine Chacón 1861–1902. 'He lived life without fear. He faced death without fear. *Muy Bravo Hombre*.'"

The *Arizona Silver Belt* and the *Bisbee Daily Review* praised Chacón's nerve on the gallows, with the former saying, "He went to his death without showing the slightest symptom of fear," and the latter stating, "Chacón met his death bravely." the *Daily Review* quoted the condemned as saying, "I consider this to be the greatest day of my life." Said the reporter for the *Graham Guardian*, with sincere admiration, "A nervier man than Augustin Chacón never walked to the gallows, and his hanging was a melodramatic spectacle that will never be forgotten by those who witnessed it."

Muy bravo hombre, indeed.[60]

Even after his death, Chacón continued to be vilified by the press, as though they were desperately attempting to justify his execution. The *Holbrook Argus* stated that Chacón had slain twenty-three men in his career but did not name any of these men he was purported to have killed or provide any further details. The *Copper Era* alleged that the Mexican consul, *Señor* Mascareñas, told "some citizens of Solomonville that Chacón had confessed to him of having killed fifteen Americans and thirty-seven Mexicans." This purported "confession," for which there is no record past its mention in the *Copper Era*, continues to be repeated by modern authors as an incontrovertibly authentic admission.

"When the spirit of Augustin Chacón was liberated from this earthly tenement," said the *Arizona Republican*, "was ended the career of one of the blackest-hearted villains that ever operated in the southwest or anywhere else. His known crimes are many, and those attributed to him almost numberless. He is said to have killed ten to twenty men, and sometimes in circumstances that would be deemed needlessly cruel even by those who value human life cheaply." The Phoenix newspaper went on to recount the killing of Pablo Salcido. Ironically, a few months later, the *Republican* recanted, saying, "Though his crimes were numerous, and many of them were perhaps are unknown, [Chacón] has been no doubt been made the scapegoat for others on more than one occasion and murders have been laid at his door of which he was not guilty."[61]

AFTERWORD

Augustine Chacón had only been in the grave about three years when *Pearson's Magazine* resurrected him. The January 1905 issue of said periodical included an exposé on the life of Captain Burt Mossman, authored by William MacLeod Raine. As might be expected, Chacón figured prominently in Mossman's story. Raine spuriously stated that Chacón "had a known record of killing twenty-eight persons, and doubtlessly many unknown victims had fallen by his rifle," as well as labeled him "the leader of the worst gang of outlaws that had ever infested the border." It is probable that Raine's primary source was Mossman himself, and it is known that the ex-Ranger captain was a bit of a braggart and not adverse to self-aggrandizement. He was also a racist.

Historian Richard White, author of the seminal book *It's Your Misfortune and None of My Own*, posited, "Virtually all nineteenth century white Americans were racially prejudiced—that is, they thought that non-whites were inferior to white." It can safely be stated that the majority of the English-language newspapers editors in the Arizona Territory were of Anglo-European descent. Further, most of them, if they were not outright racists, held strong racialist views. What they wrote and printed in their newspapers, especially in regards to Augustine Chacón, reflected their inherent prejudices. This thesis is validated by the articles examined in this study, which, if not exhibiting blatantly racist rhetoric, certainly demonstrate a marked predisposition toward racism.

The author at the grave of Augustine Chacón in San Jose, Arizona. *Author's collection.*

Direct evidence of racialist and/or racist ideologies in primary sources may not be overt and, for the neophyte historian, may not be immediately apparent. Blatant examples of racism are "often hard to come by, especially since businessmen, politicians, and editors rarely committed the innermost thoughts or plans to paper," observed Thomas Sheridan, author of *Los Tucsonenses*. "Institutionalized subordination of Mexicans…was not a conscious conspiracy" and was often "masked by a range of ideological justifications running the gamut from outright racism to well-meaning paternalism." Sheridan deduced, "[I]t is therefore necessary to draw conclusions from evidence which is often indirect or ambiguous, [and] to make inferences from the lack of available information…in the standard historical sources."[62]

Most of the articles published by modern authors utilize these old newspaper articles and memoirs as source material. Many of the stories that are disseminated in the modern publications can be traced directly back to newspaper articles that were published during Chacón's lifetime. It stands to reason, then, that if these modern authors are using these old newspapers and memoirs as their sources of information, written by newspapermen and memoirists who were racialists and/or racists, these modern authors are inadvertently (we should hope) propagating and promoting the racialist beliefs and racist agendas of those persons they utilize as their sources. To promote the legend that was founded on racist ideals is to necessarily promote the racist ideals on which the legend was founded.

It is earnestly hoped by this author that unless some new evidence or documentation is discovered, such as his military service record or an arrest warrant or indictment for any one of the fifty-two murders he has been alleged to have committed, this book will be the last word on Augustine Chacón and the legend that surrounds him will be exposed for xenophobic fabrication it is. It is hoped that he has now been vindicated.

NOTES

Chapter 1

1. "The Story True," *Graham Guardian*, December 27, 1895, 1. The original news story, as printed in this issue of the *Graham Guardian*, was rife with misinformation and inaccuracies. By way of examples, the newspaper reported that it was about noon and that Becker was at lunch when the men broke into the store, that the three men were hiding in a tent when Deputy Davis approached and that only one of the three suspects was killed in the firefight. Where possible, the author corrected these misstatements utilizing the sworn testimony from *Territory of Arizona v. Augustine Chacón*, 1896; Cliff Hanger, ed., "The Chacón Gang," *Brimstone Gazette*, November 2016, http://www.brimstonepistoleros.com/gazette/index.html; Christine Marin, "Agustine Chacón," unpublished 1982 manuscript held in Chicano/a Research Collection Small Manuscripts, 1891–2010, MM CHSM 750-MM CHSM 921, Container 898: Augustine Chacón, Arizona State University Libraries, Department of Archives and Special Collections.
2. "Escape of Chacón," *Arizona Republican*, June 11, 1897, 5; "W.A. Gillespie Went…," *Arizona Republican*, June 27, 1897, 4; Jan Cleere, *Outlaw Tales of Arizona: True Stories of Arizona's Most Famous Robbers, Rustlers, and Bandits* (Guilford, CT: Globe Pequot Press, 2006), 66. Cleere cites Harold L. Edwards and Colin Rickards in her bibliography for her chapter on Augustine Chacón; R. Michael Wilson, *Legal Executions in the Western*

Territories, 1847–1911: Arizona, Colorado, Idaho, Kansas, Montana, Nebraska, Nevada, New Mexico, North Dakota, Oklahoma, Oregon, South Dakota, Utah, Washington and Wyoming (Jefferson, NC: McFarland & Company, 2005), 43–44; Benjamin W. Olney, January 20, 1935, 5155, State File # 3715, California Death Index, 1905–39 (database online), California Department of Health and Welfare, California Vital Records, via ancestry.com; "George A. Olney Dies in New York Hospital at 66," *Arizona Republican*, May 3, 1927, 11.

3. Walter Noble Burns, *Tombstone: Iliad of the Southwest* (Garden City, NY: Doubleday & Company, 1951), 236–38; Allen A. Erwin, *The Southwest of John Horton Slaughter* (Spokane, WA: Arthur H. Clark Company, 1965), 230–36. Erwin does include Burns's book in his bibliography.
4. Glenn Burgess, ed., *Mt. Graham Profiles*, vol. 2, Ryder Ridgway Collection (Safford, AZ: Graham County Historical Society, 1988), 14, 192, 202–7, 228–29; "Story True"; "Landed in Jail," *Graham Guardian*, December 27, 1895, 1.
5. "$200 for Chacón," *Tombstone Weekly Epitaph*, June 13, 1897, 4; Mary Kay Vaughn, "Primary Education and Literacy in Nineteenth-Century Mexico: Research Trends, 1868–1988," *Latin American Research Review* 25, no. 1 (1990): 31–66; "Story True" and "Landed in Jail," 1.

Chapter 2

6. Colin Rickards, "The Hairy One: Arizona's Deadliest Bandit," *The West* (December 1970): 30–31, 56–64. Information on the town of Solomonville is derived from *Southwest Jewish History* 2, no. 4 "Solomonville: A Jewish Town on the Frontier in Arizona Territory; The Memoirs of Anne Freudenthal Solomon" (Summer 1994), https://swja.library.arizona.edu/content/solomonville; Byrd H. Granger, *Will C. Barnes' Arizona Place Names* (Tucson: University of Arizona Press, 1973), 132; Elizabeth Lantin Ramenofsky, "Isadore and Anna Solomon of Arizona: A Picture Story," *Western States Jewish History* 17, no. 2 (n.d.).
7. "Story True," 1.
8. "Court Notes," *Graham Guardian*, April 24, 1896, 1; "In the District Court," *Graham Guardian*, May 1, 1896, 1. Biographical information on Justice Owen T. Rouse was derived primarily from John S. Goff, *Arizona Territorial Officials*, vol. 1, *The Supreme Court Justices, 1863–1912* (Cave Creek, AZ: Black Mountain Press, 1975), 142–45.

9. *Territory of Arizona v. Augustine Chacón*, 1896, Graham County RG 104, SG 8, Series 3, Box 2, Case 515, Archives and Records Management Division, Arizona State Library, Archives and Public Records; Thomas H. Kramer, Robert Buckhout and Paul Eugenio, "Weapon Focus, Arousal, and Eyewitness Memory: Attention Must Be Paid," *Law and Human Behavior* 14, no. 2 (1990): 167–84, https://doi.org/10.1007/BF01062971.
10. "The Case of Augustive [*sic*] Chacón…," *Graham Guardian*, May 29, 1896, 1; "Sentenced to Be Hanged," *Graham Guardian*, June 5, 1896, 1; *Territory of Arizona v. Augustine Chacón*.

Chapter 3

11. *Territory of Arizona v. Augustine Chacón*.
12. "Tucson Entertains a Murderer," *Arizona Daily Star*, June 3, 1896, 4; "Agustin [*sic*] Chacón…," *Arizona Weekly Citizen*, July 25, 1896, 4. The man in the photograph with Chacón has been previously identified as "Juan Chavez." The back of the photos, held by the Arizona Historical Society (#29909 and #9888), indicate that Chavez was a "murderer" and "escaped from Pima County jail at Tucson. Sheriff Wakefield pursued him and shot him over toward the Santa Rita mountains." This story could not be verified.
13. "The Chacón Case," *Graham County Bulletin*, July 31, 1896, 3; *Territory of Arizona v. Augustine Chacón*; "The Supreme Court," *Arizona Republican*, January 10, 1897, 1; "Opening of the Supreme Court," *Arizona Republican*, January 12, 1897, 1.
14. "The Highest Tribunal," *Arizona Republican*, January 14, 1897, 1; "Local News of the Week," *Graham Guardian*, January 22, 1897, 1; *United States of America, Plaintiff and Respondent, v. Chung Sing, Defendant and Appellant*, 4 Ariz. 217, 36 Pac. 205, *Criminal* 92 (January 26, 1894), Caselaw Access Project, https://case.law.
15. "Supreme Court," *Arizona Republican*, February 24, 1897, 1; *Territory of Arizona v. Augustine Chacón*.
16. "About the City," *Arizona Daily Star*, April 23, 1897, 4; "Sentence to Hang," *Graham County Bulletin*, April 30, 1897, 3; Jennie Parks Ringgold, *Frontier Days in the Southwest: Pioneer Days in Old Arizona* (San Antonio, TX: Naylor Company, 1952); Joseph Miller, *Arizona: The Last Frontier* (New York: Hastings House Publishers, 1956); Harold L. Edwards, "This Is the

Greatest Day of My Life: The Hanging of Augustin Chacón," *True West* (November 1995): 14–21.

17. "Made His Escape," *Graham Guardian*, June 11, 1897, 1; "Escape of Chacón"; "Judge Rouse in Sentencing…" and "At Solomonville…," *Arizona Republican*, May 2, 1897, 4, 5; Jay J. Wagoner, *Arizona Territory 1863–1912: A Political History* (Tucson: University of Arizona Press, 1970), 329; *Acts, Resolutions, and Memorials of the Nineteenth Legislative Assembly of the Territory of Arizona* (Phoenix, AZ: Herald Book and Job Print, 1897), 51–52; "City and County in Brief," *Arizona Republican*, May 2, 1897, 5; "Who Does It Shield?," *Arizona Sentinel*, May 1, 1897, 3; "Arizona's Defective Law," *San Francisco Call*, May 5, 1897, 4; "Boon for Arizona Murderers," *San Francisco Call*, May 11, 1897, 4; "In the Case of…," *Arizona Silver Belt*, April 15, 1897, 1; "Richard Cross…," *Arizona Republican*, June 29, 1897, 5; "The Enactment of the…," *Arizona Republican*, May 18, 1897, 4.

18. "Chacón Must Die," *Arizona Republican*, June 10, 1897, 5; *Territory of Arizona v. Augustine Chacón*. Unfortunately, Wiley's letter to the governor, the petition for clemency and the missive, authored by Judge Rouse and addressed to the governor, appear to have been lost or misplaced.

19. "There Is a Report…," *Arizona Republican*, May 23, 1897, 4.

Chapter 4

20. "Pleading for Chacón," *Arizona Republican*, June 9, 1897, 5; "Attorney McCollum…" and "Chacón Must Die," *Arizona Republican*, June 10, 1897, 5.

21. "Escape of Chacón"; "Chacón Has Fled," *Graham County Bulletin*, June 11, 1897, 3; "An Enveloping Snore," *Arizona Republican*, June 16, 1897, 5; "There Will Be No Hanging," *Arizona Silver Belt*, June 17, 1897, 2; Trimble, *Arizoniana: Stories from Old Arizona* (Phoenix, AZ: Golden West Publishers, 1988), 59–60. Trimble's account would seem to have been directly influenced by Thomas E. Way, *Frontier Arizona* (New York: Carlton Press/A Milestone Book, 1960), 172, 186–87. This is a prime example of how these modern authors continue to rely on spurious secondary sources material in their works; "Made His Escape"; "Chacón Is Gone," *Graham County Bulletin*, June 18, 1897, 3; "Chacón Is Worth $700," *Arizona Republican*, June 12, 1897, 4; "Owing to the…," *Florence Tribune*, June 26, 1897, 2.

22. "Sawed His Way Out of Prison," *San Francisco Call*, June 11, 1879, 4; "Murderer Escaped," *El Paso Times*, June 11, 1897, 1; "Believed They Saw Chacón," *Graham Guardian*, June 18, 1897, 1; "W.A. Gillespie Went…," *Arizona Republican*, June 27, 1897, 4.
23. "A Desperate Fight," *Graham Guardian*, September 10, 1897, 1; "John Miller Was Murdered," *Phoenix Weekly Herald*, September 16, 1897, 4 (originally appeared in the *Graham County Bulletin*); "The Governor's Office…," *Holbrook Argus*, September 25, 1897, 10; "The Lordsburg Liberal…," *Arizona Republican*, October 10, 1897, 4; "The Liberal Is Informed…," *Graham Guardian*, October 15, 1897, 2.
24. "Mexican Horse Thieves," *Tombstone Prospector*, October 19, 1897, 4; "Fruitless Search," *Tombstone Prospector*, October 20, 1897, 4; "Local Notes," *Tombstone Prospector*, October 21, 1897, 4; "Territorial News," *Arizona Daily Star*, October 23, 1897, 1; "Word Was Received…," *Tombstone Prospector*, October 22, 1897, 4.
25. Lorenzo D. Walters, *Tombstone's Yesterdays* (Glorieta, NM: Rio Grande Press, 1968), 226–29; R. Michael Wilson, *Stagecoach Robbery in Arizona & New Mexico* (N.p.: self-published, 2012), 46–48.
26. "A Murder at Morenci," *Arizona Daily Citizen*, October 28, 1897, 1; "Swift Vengeance," *Tombstone Weekly Epitaph*, October 31, 1897, 4; "Last Friday Night…," *Arizona Weekly Journal-Miner*, November 3, 1897, 2.
27. "Solomanville [*sic*]," *Los Angeles Times*, September 1, 1898, 10; "In Today's Guardian…," *Graham Guardian*, August 12, 1898, 4; "Augustin Chacón…," *Western Liberal*, September 2, 1898, 3; "Arizona News," *Holbrook Argus*, September 3, 1898, 4; "Solomonville," *Los Angeles Times*, September 20, 1898, 7.
28. "Chacón Hanged," *Copper Era and Morenci Leader*, November 27, 1902, 2.

Chapter 5

29. "Editorial Notes," *Arizona Weekly Journal-Miner*, March 8, 1899, 2; "Arizona Day-by-Day," *Arizona Republican*, March 20, 1899, 3; "We Can Imagine…," *Graham Guardian*, March 24, 1899, 4; "Proclamation of Reward," *Graham Guardian*, July 2, 1897, 4; "Arizona," *El Paso Herald*, March 30, 1899, 3; "Territorial News," *Arizona Daily Star*, March 30, 1899, 4; "A Proclamation…," *Daily Orb*, April 2, 1899, 4.
30. "Arizona Day by Day," *Arizona Republican*, November 19, 1899, 3.

31. "Nogales," *Los Angeles Times*, November 27, 1899, 11; "Two Bandits Die," *Border Vidette*, October 21, 1899, 2.
32. "Murdered at Morenci," *Graham Guardian*, April 20, 1900, 1; "Murdered for Money," *El Paso Times*, April 22, 1900, 4; "Triple Murder," *El Paso Herald*, April 24, 1900, 5; "Three Chinamen Murdered," *Copper Era & Morenci Leader* 2, no. 2 (n.d.): 2; "Three Chinaman Murdered," *Evening Times*, April 25, 1900, 3; "Three Chinks," *Marion Star*, April 25, 1900, 1; "Robbers Kill Three Chinamen," *Naugatuch Daily News*, April 25, 1900, 1; "Three Chinamen Killed," *St. Louis Globe Democrat*, April 25, 1900, 4; "Three Chinamen Killed," *Owensboro Messenger-Inquirer*, April 26, 1900, 1; "Murder of Arizona Chinese," *Los Angeles Times*, April 28, 1900, 27.
33. "It Is Said…," *Arizona Silver Belt*, May 10, 1900, 8; "A Station Slaughter," *Arizona Republican*, June 9, 1900, 4; "New River Killing," *Arizona Republican*, June 10, 1900, 1; "A Desert Murder" and "In Hot Pursuit," *Arizona Weekly Journal-Miner*, June 13, 1900, 2 and 8; "Proclamation of Reward" and "Reward—$800," *Arizona Republican*, June 13, 1900, 3; "The New River Murders," *Florence Tribune*, June 16, 1900, 3; "Augustin Chacón…" and "Trailing the Outlaws," *Arizona Republican*, June 18, 1900, 1 and 5; Bandits Said to Have Been Slain," *San Francisco Chronicle*, June 20, 1900, 10; "Sheriff's Posse Still After the Murderers," *Tucson Citizen*, June 21, 1900, 1; "An Arizona Outlaw," *The Tombstone Epitaph*, June 24, 1900, 1; "Chacón Heard From," *Graham Guardian*, June 22, 1900, 1.
34. "Deputy Sheriff Jas. Nicks Came…," *Western Liberal*, June 22, 1900, 3; "Gaspar Garcia and Pedro Herrera…," *Copper Era and Morenci Leader*, June 28, 1900, 2; "In the District Court," *Copper Era and Morenci Leader*, October 18, 1900, 4; "A Band of Desperadoes…," *Copper Era and Morenci Leader*, June 28, 1900, 4; "Two Men Foully Murdered Near Morenci," *Graham Guardian*, July 20, 1900, 1; "The News of Jerome," *Arizona Republican*, July 22, 1900, 7; "The News of Jerome," *Arizona Republican*, July 26, 1900, 3; "Graham County Officers Out After Murderers," *Arizona Daily Citizen*, July 28, 1900, 1; "A Determined Posse," *Arizona Republican*, July 29, 1900, 6; William MacLeod Raine, "Carrying Law into the Mesquite," *Pearson's Magazine* 13, no. 1 (January 1905): 69–77; James H. McClintock, *Arizona, Prehistoric, Aboriginal, Pioneer, Modern—The Nation's Youngest Commonwealth within a Land of Ancient Culture* (Chicago: S.J. Clarke Publishing Company, 1916), 470; Ringgold, *Frontier Days*, 139; Rickards, "Hairy One," 56; Cleere, *Outlaw Tales of Arizona*, 66; Laurence J. Yandon and Dan Anderson, *Arizona Gunfighters*, ed. Robert Barr Smith (New Orleans, LA: Pelican Publishing Company, 2010), 238; Erin Turner, ed., *Outlaw Tales of the Old*

West: Fifty True Stories of Desperados, Crooks, Criminals, and Bandits (Lanham, MD: Rowman & Littlefield, 2016), 35.

35. "Saw Chacón," *Arizona Republican*, July 29, 1900, 5; "An Arizona Bandit," *Missoulian*, June 23, 1900, 3; "Announcement," *Graham Guardian*, August 10, 1900, 4; "First Catch Your Hare," *Arizona Republican*, July 30, 1900, 5; "It Is Reported…." *Western Liberal*, August 3, 1900, 2 and 4; "To Exterminate Bandits," *Fitchburg Sentinel*, July 30, 1900, 8; "A Bandit Chase," *Printer*, August 1, 1900, 7; "Arizona Brevities," *Los Angeles Times*, August 14, 1900, 5; "Chacón, the Morenci Murderer…," *Western Liberal*, August 31, 1900, 3.
36. "Three Men Killed," *Graham Guardian*, September 21, 1900, 1; "Murdered for Their Money," *Holbrook Argus*, September 22, 1900, 2; "Murdered in Their Tent," *San Francisco Chronicle*, September 16, 1900, 5; "Tragedy in Arizona," *Los Angeles Times*, September 27, 1900, 12; "Donaciano Corona Charged…," *Los Angeles Sunday Times*, October 21, 1900, part 4, 29; "In the District Court," *Copper Era*, November 1, 1900, 4; Donaciano Corona, Inmate #1687, Inmate Register & Description List, Yuma Prison Records, Territory of Arizona, 1900–1909, file film #23.1.17, held at the Arizona State Library, Archives, and Public Records.
37. "Headless Corpse Found," *Los Angeles Times*, November 25, 1900, 3; "Headless Corpse Found," *Holbrook Argus*, December 1, 1900, 2; "Solomonville (A.T.)," *San Francisco Chronicle*, December 9, 1900, 3; "Juan Hernandez and Jesus Lerma…," *Holbrook Argus*, December 15, 1900, 2.

Chapter 6

38. "Burt Alvord…," *Tombstone Prospector*, December 22, 1899, 4. Biographical information on Burt Alvord in this chapter was derived primarily from Don Chaput, *The Odyssey of Burt Alvord* (Tucson, AZ: Westernlore Press, 2000); "On Monday…," *Cochise Review*, January 19, 1901, 2; "At Naco…," *Los Angeles Times*, January 24, 10; "Outlaw Gang May Raid Tombstone," *San Francisco Chronicle*, January 27, 1901, 4.
39. "Bold Train Robbery," *Arizona Republican*, September 11, 1899, 4; "Saturday Night…," *The Oasis*, September 16, 1899, 7; "A Hold Up," *The Tombstone Epitaph*, February 18, 1900, 1; "Train No. 1…," *Holbrook Argus*, February 24, 1900, 4; "Three Finger Jack," "More Prisoner's Captured," "Another Capture," "Bravo John in Jail" and "Sensational Arrests," *The Tombstone Epitaph*, February 25, 1900, 1, 2 and 4; "Sensational Evidence,"

Florence Tribune, March 10, 1900, 3; "Break Jail," *Arizona Daily Orb*, April 7, 1900, 4; "At Their Old Haunts" and "The Willcox News…," *Florence Tribune*, May 5, 1900, 1 and 3; "Stiles Surrenders," *Cochise Review*, July 2, 1900, 1; "Cut Out Stiles," *Cochise Review*, December 22, 1900, 4; "All the Indictments…," *Cochise Review*, December 22, 1900, 3. Much of the biographical information on Burton C. Mossman in this chapter was derived from Robert H. Carlock, *The Hashknife: The Early Days of the Aztec Land and Cattle Company, Limited* (Tucson, AZ: Westernlore Press, 1994), 281–98; D.L. Turner, "Arizona's Twenty-Four Hour War: The Arizona Rangers and the Cananea Copper Strike of 1906," *Journal of Arizona History* 48, no. 3 (Autumn 2007): 257–88.

40. "Alvord Again," *Cochise Review*, March 9, 1901, 6; "The Reported Visit…" and "Still After Alvord," *Tombstone Weekly Epitaph*, March 10, 1901, 1; "Henry Shwink…," *Arizona Silver Belt*, April 25, 1901, 5 (the man *The Epitaph* named as "Frank Swink" was identified in the *Silver Belt* as "Henry Shwink"; the author, basing his opinion on the lack of mention of a "Shwink" in the territorial press, is inclined to believe that the first is the man's true name); "The Sheriff and His Posse…," *Arizona Republican*, March 13, 1901, 3; "In Many Places," *Arizona Republican*, March 14, 1901, 3; "Nothing Further…" & "We Have Heard…," *Tombstone Weekly Epitaph*, March 17, 1901, 1 and 2.
41. "Alvord," *Arizona Daily Star*, March 30, 1901, 1; "Chacón with Alvord," *Tombstone Weekly Epitaph*, April 7, 1901, 3; "Two Noted Desperados," *Arizona Weekly Journal-Miner*, April 10, 1901, 2; "It Was Reported…," *Florence Tribune*, 2; "After Outlaws," *Graham Guardian*, May 3, 1901, 4.
42. "Alvord Seen," *Tombstone Weekly Epitaph*, July 14, 1901, 2; "Johnson in the Toils," *The Tombstone Epitaph*, November 3, 1901, 4; "Brief News of the Town," *Arizona Daily Citizen*, November 27, 1901, 4; "The Alvord Story," *Arizona Republican*, December 2, 1901, 5; "Chacón Hanged," *Copper Era & Morenci Leader*, November 27, 1902, 2.
43. "Doom of Arizona Bandits," *El Paso Times*, January 14, 1902, 19. Arizona Ranger Carlos Tafolla and tracker Bill Maxwell, who were killed in a shootout with the Bill Smith Gang in October 1901, are likely the men alluded to in the article; "After Famous Arizona Murderer," *Tucson Citizen*, February 1, 1902, 5; "Burt Alvord Seen in Cananea," *Bisbee Daily Review*, January 11, 1902, 3; "Local and Personal," *Bisbee Daily Review*, 4.
44. "A Great Haul," *Graham Guardian*, April 11, 1902, 1; "Sheriff Parks of Graham…," *Western Liberal*, April 11, 1902, 2; "Cattle Thieves Captured," *Arizona Sentinel*, April 9, 1902, 3.

45. "Rangers Are Hot After Noted Fugitive from Justice," *Bisbee Daily Review*, April 27, 1902, 6; "Rangers After Fugitive," *Arizona Daily Star*, April 30, 1902, 6; "Man Tried, Should Have Been Bound Over," *Bisbee Daily Review*, April 30, 1902, 1; "Will Hunt Noted Bandit," May 2, 1902, 1; "Has Killed Forty-Two Men," *Pittsburgh Press*, May 16, 1902, 16. The *Pittsburgh Press* credited the article to "Phoenix correspondence. San Francisco Examiner." The author was unable to find the original source article.
46. "Noted Desperado Cleverly Captured," *Tucson Citizen*, September 4, 1902, 1; "Chacón Captured," *Copper Era*, September 4, 1902, 3; "Importans [*sic*] Capture," *Arizona Daily Star*, September 5, 1902, 5; "Capture of Chacón the Bloodiest Criminal," *Arizona Republican*, September 5, 1902, 1; "Augustin Chacón Is Captured," *Bisbee Daily Review*, September 5, 1902, 4.
47. "Petition for Removal" and "Another Statement," *Bisbee Daily Review*, August 19, 1902, 9; "City Police vs. Rangers," *Bisbee Daily Review*, August 17, 1902, 8; "Captain Mossman Has Resigned," *Bisbee Daily Review*, August 20, 1902, 5; "Tom Ryning [*sic*] Notified," *Bisbee Daily Review*, August 22, 1902, 4.
48. "Personal Mention," *Bisbee Daily Review*, September 6, 1902, 1; "Noted Outlaw and Murderer," *The Tombstone Epitaph*, September 7, 1902, 1; "Details of Chacón's Capture," *Bisbee Daily Review*, September 7, 1902, 4; "Brief City News," *Bisbee Daily Review*, September 10, 1902, 8; "Chacón Captured," *Arizona Sentinel*, September 10, 1902, 3; "Augustin Chacón Captured," *Arizona Silver Belt*, September 11, 1902, 3; "The Era Was Misinformed…," *Copper Era*, September 11, 1902, 2.
49. "Burt Alvord," *Tucson Citizen*, September 11, 1902, 5; "Burt Alvord in Custody" and "Shoots 'em Up," *Bisbee Daily Review*, September 12, 1902, 1 and 5; "Augustin Chacón Forfeits His Life," *Graham Guardian*, November 28, 1902, 1; "Inside History of Alvord's Arrest," *Copper Era*, September 18, 1902, 3.
50. Burgess, *Mt. Graham Profiles*, 204–5; "Story of the Capture," *Graham Guardian*, September 12, 1902, 1.
51. "Alvord's Case Dismissed," *Bisbee Daily Review*, December 2, 1902, 5; "All Charges Dismissed," *Arizona Daily Star*, December 4, 1902, 1; "Burt Alvord Has Plead Guilty," *Bisbee Daily Review*, December 9, 1903, 1; "Stiles and Alvord Again Break Jail," *Arizona Daily Star*, December 16, 1903, 1; "Alvord Captured After Being Shot," *Bisbee Daily Review*, February 20, 1904, 1; "Burt Alvord in Jail," *Arizona Republican*, February 21, 1904, 1; "Alvord Has Been Taken…," *Arizona Daily Star*, February 24, 1904, 4;

"Alvord Is Taken to Pen in Yuma," *Bisbee Daily Review*, March 5, 1904, 8; "The Story of Bravo Juan, Alvord, and 'Billy' Stiles," *Arizona Daily Star*, March 20, 1910, 28; Chaput, *Odyssey of Burt Alvord*, 134.

52. "Are Together," *Bisbee Daily Review*, April 12, 1906, 8; "Have Located Stiles," *Bisbee Daily Review*, April 19, 1906, 3; "Outlaws Plan Bold Raid in Yuma," *Bisbee Daily Review*, August 15, 1906, 8; "Arizona Outlaws Seen in Sonora," *Arizona Republican*, January 25, 1907, 3; "Billy Stiles Has Perished by Violence," *Bisbee Daily Review*, December 19, 1908, 1; "Killing of Billy Stiles Corroborated by Letter to Review from His Wife," *Bisbee Daily Review*, December 20, 1908, 1; "The Notorious Bandit William Larkin Stiles Still an Uncertainty," *Arizona Daily Star*, August 8, 1909, 1–2, 6; "Deputy Sheriff William Larkin Stiles," American Peace Officer Museum, https://peaceofficersmuseum.org/2015/05/deputy-sheriff-william-larkin-stiles; "William Larkin Stiles," James D. Hoff Peace Officer Memorial, from article reprinted from the *Humboldt Star*, December 7, 1908, http://www.hoffmemorial.org/enshrined-officers/william-larkin-stiles.

53. Carlock, *Hashknife*, 281–98; "Change in Firm," *Bisbee Daily Review*, October 25, 1902, 8; "Captain Burton C. Mossman…," *Holbrook Argus*, November 14, 1903, 5; "Captain Mossman Married," *Arizona Republican*, December 9, 1905, 7; "Mossman Shipped East Sixty Odd Cars Cattle," *Bisbee Daily Review*, May 26, 1906, 3.

Chapter 7

54. "Outlawry in Arizona," *Bisbee Daily Review*, September 19, 1902, 2; "District Court Is…," *Bisbee Daily Review*, October 7, 1902, 2.

55. "He Will Have to Hang for His Crime," *Oakland Tribune*, September 4, 1902, 2; "Border Bandit Again Jailed," *Los Angeles Daily Times*, September 12, 1902, part 2, 6; "Slayer of 23 Men Is Caught," *Boston Post*, September 15, 1902, 8; "Alvord Loses His Nerve," *San Francisco Chronicle*, September 12, 1902, 3; "Burt Alvord in Custody," *Los Angeles Times*, September 12, 1901, part 1, 3. Especially remarkable among the national newspapers that featured stories about Chacón's arrest is the *San Francisco Examiner*'s full-page exposé in the September 21, 1902 edition.

56. "Local News of the Week," *Graham Guardian*, October 10, 1902, 1; "Augustin Chacón Will Hang," October 12, 1902, 1; "Chacón Sentenced to Hang," *Copper Era*, October 16, 1902, 3; "Chacón to Hang," *Arizona*

Silver Belt, October 23, 1902, 6; "The Hanging of Chacón," *Arizona Republican*, November 7, 1902, 4.

57. "Sheriff Parks Has Issued…," *Copper Era*, November 13, 1902, 2; Burgess, *Mt. Graham Profiles*, 205; Ringgold, *Frontier Days*, 144; "Agustin [*sic*] Chacón Will Hang," *Bisbee Daily Review*, November 18, 1902, 1; Vaughn, "Primary Education and Literacy," 31–66.

58. "Gus Chacón," *Tucson Citizen*, November 20, 1902, 5; "Trying to Save Chacón," *Bisbee Daily Review*, November 21, 1902, 1; "Efforts to Release Chacón," *Graham Guardian*, November 21, 1902, 3; BlackPast, "(1905) Theodore Roosevelt, 'Lincoln and the Race Problem,'" https://www.blackpast.org/african-american-history/1905-theodore-roosevelt-lincoln-and-race-problem-3; "Nogales Notes," *The Oasis*, November 29, 1902, 5.

59. "Augustin Chacón Forfeits His Life," *Graham Guardian*, November 28, 1902, 1; "Chacón Pays Death Penalty," *Bisbee Daily Review*, November 22, 1902, 1; Catherine Hellier and Robert Connolly, "Cause of Death in Judicial Hanging: A Review and Case Study," *Medicine, Science, and the Law* 49 (January 2009): 18–26, 10.1258/rsmmsl.49.1.18; Richard Clark, "Hanged by the Neck Until Dead!: The Processes and Physiology of Judicial Hanging," Capital Punishment U.K., 1995, http://www.capitalpunishmentuk.org/hanging2.html.

60. Ringgold, *Frontier Days*, 144; Burgess, *Mt. Graham Profiles*, 206; "Chacón Hanged Last Friday," *Arizona Silver Belt*, November 27, 1902, 4; "Chacón Pays Death Penalty," *Bisbee Daily Review*, November 22, 1902, 1; "Augustin Chacón Forfeits His Life," *Graham Guardian*, November 28, 1902, 1.

61. "Gallows Awaits Man Slayer," *Holbrook Argus*, November 29, 1902, 6; "Chacón Hanged," *Copper Era & Morenci Leader*, November 27, 1902, 2, "Chacón Died Gamely Protesting His Innocence," *Arizona Republican*, November 22, 1902, 1 (the *Republican* named the Catholic priest who visited Chacón in his final hours as "DeRichermont," the *Daily Review* named him as "Derichmond" and the *Graham Guardian* named him as "Dertchement"; the author was unable to locate any more information on the man under any of these names); Augustine "Peludo" Chacón, San Jose Cemetery, San Jose, Graham County, Arizona, Memorial I.D. 24403261, Find A Grave, https://www.findagrave.com/memorial/24403261#; "Chacón Died Gamely Protesting Innocence," *Arizona Republican*, November 22, 1902, 3.

Afterword

62. Raine, "Carrying Law into the Mesquite," 69–77; "An Arizona Story," *Arizona Republican*, December 27, 1904, 71–77; Richard White, *"It's Your Misfortune and None of My Own": A History of the American West* (Norman: University of Oklahoma Press, 1991), 321; Thomas E. Sheridan, *Los Tucsoneneses: The Mexican Community in Tucson, 1854–1941* (Tucson: University of Arizona Press, 1997), 6–7.

ABOUT THE AUTHOR

Photograph by Patricia Sullivan.

David Grassé, the son of Walter and Geraldine Grassie, is a third-generation Arizonian, being born in Casa Grande and raised in Tucson. He currently resides in the town of Payson, in Arizona's rim country. Grassé possesses both an undergraduate degree in history and a master's degree in information resources and library science from the University of Arizona. He is a member of the Arizona Historical Society, the Western Writers of America and the Arizona Library Association. Grassé has two previously published books to his name and has authored several magazine, journal and newspaper articles, all relating to the territorial period in Arizona, more specifically criminality, law enforcement and the judicial system of said era. He remains employed as a reference librarian because writing western history does not pay the bills.